Psychology of Persuasion

Secrets to Influence People & Human Behavior with Dark Cognitive Therapy CBT, Emotional Intelligence. Win Friends using Social Leverage, Empathy and Business Relationship Skills

BLAKE CODE

© Copyright 2019 - All rights reserved.

PSYCHOLOGY OF PERSUASION
First edition. October 2019.
Copyright © 2019 Blake Code.
Written by Blake Code.

Table of Contents

Introduction

Congratulations for purchasing *Psychology of Persuasion: Secrets to Influence People & Human Behavior with Dark Cognitive Therapy CBT, Emotional Intelligence. Win Friends Using Social Leverage, Empathy, and Business Relationship Skills,* and thanks for doing so.

The following chapters will discuss how you can use persuasion to improve all aspects of your life, whether it's your personal relationships, career prospects, professional relationships, or standing in your community.

The book will examine the psychodynamic history of persuasion, as well as its roots in philosophy. We will examine strategies that can be used to persuade people in all walks of life, and how you can use Aristotle's rhetoric techniques to make a convincing argument at any time.

The book will also delve into the connection between persuasion and effective communication. We will look at what you can do to develop communication skills, and we will discuss various rhetoric tools that can make you a more persuasive communicator.

We will look at the dark triad traits that are characteristic of most manipulators, and from that, we will draw lessons on how you can be more persuasive without being malicious.

We will also explore the concept of emotional intelligence and illustrate why it's important if you want to succeed in life. You will learn the 5 essential abilities that characterize emotional intelligence and what you can do to internalize those abilities.

The book will also teach you how to read people and decipher their emotions in order to increase your persuasiveness, and how you can use your own emotional intelligence to affect other people's behavior.

We will also explore cognitive behavioral therapy (CBT) and teach you various techniques that can help you rectify your mindset.

Towards the end, we will discuss various crucial social skills, and how you can acquire them if you want to increase your chances of success in business and in life.

There are lots of books on persuasion in the market right now, so thank you very much for choosing this one! Every effort was made to ensure that this book is filled with useful information and insights that can help you improve your life, so please enjoy!

CHAPTER 1:

The History of Persuasion

The study of persuasion is one of the oldest disciplines known to man. In fact, philosophers and other academics have been studying effective communication and other aspects of persuasion for more than 2500 years, according to historical records. In this chapter, we will look at the psychodynamic history of persuasion, as well as how the concept of persuasion was portrayed in Greek mythology.

Psychodynamic History of Persuasion

Plato famously defined persuasion as the art of winning the soul by discourse. We will take a deeper look at the way Philosophers (particularly Aristotle) broke down the concept of persuasion in the next chapter.

From a psychodynamic perspective, persuasion involves both a logical and emotional concept. In other words, to successfully persuade someone, psychologists believe that you have to appeal to both the way they think and the way they feel.

For more than 100 years, psychologists have understood that persuasion goes beyond conscious awareness. Sigmund Freud was among the first psychologists to point out that the conscious mind is just the tip of the iceberg, and that if you wanted to effectively influence someone's thinking, you would have to utilize techniques that affect not just the person's conscious awareness, but also his or her subconscious mind.

The psychodynamic understanding of persuasion is also impacted by our understanding of evolution. From Darwin's theory of evolution, we understand that we are hardwired to survive, and that means acting out of self-interest. You can persuade people more effectively if you understand what their interests are. In other words, to effectively persuade someone you have to incentivize them; you can offer them something they need, or you can threaten them with something they fear.

Persuasion is also about language and other forms of communication. You can persuade people more effectively if you are good at using words, vocal cues, and non-verbal signals. Scholars, philosophers, and early psychologists believe that we are more persuasive if we communicate in a more articulate and confident manner. Anthropologists in the 19th century also figured out that body language has a lot of impact on how effective we were at communicating, and persuasion by extension.

Persuasion in Greek Mythology

In Greek mythology, persuasion was such an important concept that it was personified as a god. Peitho was the goddess of persuasion and seduction. The true ancestry of the goddess Peitho is unclear, but she is closely associated with Aphrodite, the goddess of love, beauty, pleasure, procreation, and passion. It's significant that Peitho works so closely with Aphrodite (some ancient texts have even indicated that Peitho might be Aphrodite's daughter), because persuasion as a concept, goes hand in hand with many of the traits that Aphrodite embodies.

The goddess of persuasion, Peitho, rarely plays a central character in the stories about the Greek gods, but she often makes an appearance in wherever persuasion is pivotal to the plot of a story. For example, most artistic depictions of the story of Helen and Paris feature Peitho.

You are probably familiar with the story of Helen, Paris, and Troy; but you may not be aware of the role of the goddess Peitho in the plot of the story. To understand the importance of persuasion in Greek mythology, we will use this story as a case study.

Paris is born a prince, but there is a prophecy that indicates he will bring ruin to his people, so his parents get rid of him, and he ends up growing up as a shepherd. Despite his humble upbringing, Paris grows up to be the most handsome and well-respected person on earth, and he gains a reputation among the gods as a fair-minded ad wise you, man.

Meanwhile, a contest arises among the goddesses. There is a wedding in Zeus's palace, and all the goddesses get an invite, except one; Eris, the goddess of chaos. Eris feels snubbed, so she tosses the golden apple of discord into the palace. The apple has an inscription that says "for the fairest," so each goddess at the wedding immediately assumes it's meant for her, and the seed of discord is planted.

The goddesses compete to find out which one of them the fairest, and the price is a golden apple. After much competition, the field is narrowed down to 3 goddesses: Aphrodite (the goddess of beauty), Athena (goddess of war and wisdom) and (Hera, the goddess of marriage).

At this point, it falls on Zeus to decide which of the three goddesses is the fairest and most deserving of the golden apple. Zeus, in his wisdom, realizes that if he chooses one goddess over the others, he will have to deal with chaotic descent. He, therefore, decides that the contest will be judged by the fairest judge in the land; the wise shepherd boy, Paris.

Paris accepted the role of the judge. He met with all the 3 goddesses and carefully inspected each one of them, but he couldn't arrive at an immediate decision. While he was still deliberating on his decision, the goddesses started offering him bribes. The Goddess Hera offered Paris power. The goddess Athena offered Paris wisdom and Strength. The goddess, Aphrodite, offered Paris love: the love of the most beautiful mortal woman in all the land: that was Helen.

If you are familiar with this ancient story, you probably know that Paris ended up choosing Aphrodite as the fairest of the goddesses. However, there is a part of that story that is left out in most modern versions of the narrative, and that is the role of Peitho, the goddess of persuasion.

As we have mentioned, Peitho, was a companion of Aphrodite, and without her help, Aphrodite wouldn't have been able to beat Athena and Hera. It's easy to assume that Paris chose love instead of power, strength, and wisdom because that was in his nature (he had a reputation as a womanizer); but the more reasonable explanation for his decision could be that he was persuaded to make that choice.

Some scholars believe that Aphrodite was able to persuade Paris to forgo here's offer to make him the most powerful man on earth, and Athena's offer to make him the wisest and strongest man on earth, not because her offer of love was the best one, but because she had a secret weapon, and that was Peitho, the goddess of persuasion (most objective men today are more likely to choose wealth and power over love).

Scholars have come to believe that Peitho played two important roles in the story. First, she helped Aphrodite to convince Paris that love is better than power, wisdom, and strength. Second, she helped Aphrodite convince Helen to leave her husband Menelaus and fall in love with Paris.

From this story, you can understand how the ancient Greeks viewed persuasion. According to them, it is a powerful tool that gives whoever wields it, a great advantage over his or her competitors. Hera and Athena offered Paris offers that were just as good (or even arguably better) than Aphrodite's offer, but in the end, she triumphed over them because Peitho gave her an edge. In other words, she won because she was more persuasive.

CHAPTER 2:

Aristotle's Three Modes of Persuasion

Aristotle was a Greek (Athenian) philosopher who lived in the 4th century BC. His views of persuasion are close to 2500 years old, but they are still the foundation of our modern understanding of the concept of persuasion. Over the past couple of melena, lots of books, studies, stories, etc. have been written on persuasion, but most scholars agree that Aristotle's Treatise on Rhetoric is still the single most important body of work on the subject.

Aristotle defined analysis perception from the point of view of a rhetorician. Aristotle, like most other Greek philosophers, was a sort of educator. He would move from town to town, addressing crowds of followers. This is the same method of teaching that was used by Jesus and many other influential people back then. To Aristotle, understanding the art of persuasion was important because he needed this skill to be effective at what he did.

Aristotle believed that to be able to persuade people; one had to have "the ability to observe in any given case, the available means of persuasion." In other words, if you want to be an effective persuader, you need to have the ability to analyze the situation you are in and to correctly identify all the means of persuasion that are at your disposal at that particular moment.

Aristotle went further than that; he identified the 3 key "modes" of persuasion. According to him, these "modes" were available to every communicator, irrespective of where they were, what situation they were dealing with or even what language they spoke; these modes of persuasion were universal.

Aristotle's modes of persuasion are Ethos, Logos, and Pathos.

Ethos is the Greek word for "character," and it's the origin of the English word "ethics." It refers to the character of the speaker, and there his or her credibility.

Logos is the origin of the word "logic," and as you might imagine, it refers to rationality and reason. Being logical means that you adhere to the formal (and therefore the common) rules of thinking.

Pathos is the Greek word for "emotion," and it's the origin of the English word "empathy." It dictates that a persuasive argument has to appeal to someone's emotions.

In this chapter, we will take an in-depth look at each of the 3 modes.

Ethos

As we've mentioned, ethos relates to the communicator's credibility, character, and reputation. The idea here is that to be persuasive; you have to manage the preconceptions that your audience or targets have about you. People are often persuaded because what they think of the person who is persuading them as opposed to the information that they are receiving.

In a way, is about whether or not you come across as authoritative. People will be persuaded by what you say once you have established yourself as an authority on the subject. For example, you are more likely to take legal advice from an articulate person in an impeccable suit who identified himself or herself as a lawyer, than you are to take the same exact advice from a shaggy stranger who claims to understand the law. There is a simple reason for this; the appearance of each of these people indicates to you how credible they are. The person in a decent suit, who speaks like a trained professional seems credible. The person who dresses poorly and speaks informally doesn't seem credible.

Appearance is a vital part of the ethos, and it applies pretty much everywhere. Lots of studies show that people who dress better seem more credible. Businessmen in suits are taken more seriously than those who dress casually.

The concept of ethos is similar to the concept of first impressions. When you want to persuade someone of something, the impression you create about yourself affects whether or not that person will buy your line of argument.

Apart from physical appearance, ethos also applies to introductions. When you introduce yourself to an audience, they decide how credible you are based on that introduction. Before presenting an argument to an audience, you can increase your persuasiveness by introducing yourself in a way that makes you sound like someone who is an authority on the subject of the argument.

For example, if you find yourself in a boardroom, pitching an idea to people you are meeting for the first time, you can use ethos in your introduction by mentioning your academic background, your other qualifications, your job title, your experience, your affiliations, etc.

An entrepreneur who mentions that she has an MBA and 5 years of experience, is likely to be more persuasive than one who just mentions her name and carry on with the pitch.

Ethos based appeals can be based on the perceptions that the audience has formed about you in the past, instead of how you present yourself at the moment. People can be persuaded because the claim you are making is consistent with what you have said or done in the past. For example, if you borrow cash from a friend, he is more likely to be persuaded to give it to you if you have paid your debts to him in the past. Here, your friend finds you credible not because of your words, but because of your past actions.

The concept of ethos also explains why celebrity endorsements are so effective when it comes to marketing. When you like certain celebrities, you find them "reputable," and as a result, you ascribe them to a certain level of authority. You are, therefore, more likely to purchase products that they recommend.

Logos

Logos based appeals are about facts and figures. These appeals work because they are logical. Logos assumes that most people are reasonable. If you present someone with facts and statistics to favor your argument, they are more likely to buy it. Even in the absence of absolute facts and figures, arguments that are logical (those that are consistent with a set of agreed-upon facts and assumptions) can be used to persuade your audience.

In most court cases, the jury is often unaware of all the facts. They are presented with a set of facts that form the basis of the case; then, they are presented with two logical narratives. Often times, the jury will buy the arguments that ultimately sounds more reasonable.

It's important to note that "logos" is not necessarily based on provable scientific facts; sometimes, it can come into play in situations where all parties have a shared system of belief, even if those beliefs may seem illogical to other people. For example, members of the same religion can use logos to persuade each other of certain things, but if those same arguments were presented to outsiders, they wouldn't seem at all reasonable.

Pathos

Pathos arguments, as we've mentioned, appeal to the person's empathy. Empathy is one's ability to understand and relate to other people's feelings and experiences. It's one's ability to put himself or herself in a situation, and judge that situation depending on how he or she would feel, and what his or her values are. When you use a pathos argument, you are trying to intentionally evoke a certain emotional reaction in your audience in an attempt to persuade them.

There are 3 ways to make a pathos argument; you can create an emotional response, you can tell a convincing story, or you can make an impassioned plea.

Pathos is persuasive because it helps the audience relate to the argument that you are making. Psychologists have long understood that emotions are stronger than logic when it comes to driving our reactions. We are more likely to do what we feel than what logically think we ought to do. So, pathos is arguably a more effective persuasion modality than logos or ethos.

Remember that as a communicator, pathos is not about your own emotions; it's about the emotions of the audience. Many people misunderstand the concept of pathos; they end up assuming that they can deploy it by displaying extreme emotions, but oftentimes, that doesn't work. Crying in front of an audience might not necessarily get then to empathize with your argument, but telling an emotionally wrenching story might do the trick.

Pathos could involve invoking any emotion, whether it's negative or positive, as long as it serves your purposes. For example, if you want to convince someone to donate to a charity, you might want to invoke the feeling of compassion. However, if you want to convince the person to join the civil rights movement, you might want to invoke the feelings of anger and outrage.

Aristotle's 3 modes of persuasion work more effectively when they are used in conjunction with each other. They tend to complement each other, especially when they are used in a well-structured argument. For example, a politician trying to convince someone to vote for him might start out a brief speech by pointing out his qualifications and experience (ethos), use facts and figures to lay out his policy proposals (logos), and speak passionately about the need for change and his vision for the voters (pathos).

CHAPTER 3:

Persuasion Theories

There are many different theories of persuasion (also known as influence theories), but for our purposes, we will take a look at 3 of the most common ones: including cognitive dissonance theory, social judgment theory, and the elaboration likelihood model.

Before we explore each of the theories, let's look at what persuasion entails. In order to persuade someone, you need three things; first, you need to have a goal, as well as the intention to see that goal through. Secondly, you need a means of achieving that goal (a way to communicate with whomever you are trying to persuade). Thirdly, you need to have the component of free will (particularly on the part of the recipient).

These are important defining factors where persuasion is concerned: the implication here is that persuasion is neither accidental nor coercive. It's a simple three-step process: you decide what you want from someone, you deploy non-coercive techniques to influence that person, and the person does what you want out of freewill.

Cognitive Dissonance Theory

This theory is based on three key points. The first point is that people are wired to seek consistency in all aspects of their lives. The second pint is that people are naturally sensitive to inconsistencies, contradictions, and disorder. The point is that when people experience dissonance (which is often manifested in the form of doubt, guilt, and even discomfort), they experience a change in their attitude.

We experience dissonance when we have two different thoughts or ideas that logically contradict each other; if one is true, then the other is false. In other words, these thoughts are inconsistent.

There are several ways for people to deal with cognitive dissonance. For starters, when you have 2 different thoughts that contradict each other, you could change one of the thoughts so that it becomes consistent with the other. For example, if your first thought is "I love eating junk food" and your second thought is "junk food is detrimental to my health" you might deal with the contradiction by changing the second thought into "well, junk food isn't that bad."

The second way to deal with cognitive dissonance is to change one's behavior (if we were to use the above example, you could change your behavior by cutting down on junk food).

The third way to deal with the cognitive dissonance is to add new thoughts that somehow rationalize the contradiction between the first two thoughts (in our example above, you might rationalize eating junk food by thinking "I have an active lifestyle so the junk food won't cause me much harm").

The fourth way to deal with cognitive dissonance is to trivialize the inconsistency that is causing the dissonance. You do this by convincing yourself that the dissonance is "no big deal."

For dissonance to occur in one's mind, there are a few important conditions that have to be fulfilled. First, the person has to feel like he or she had a choice in the matter (for example, you may experience cognitive dissonance from eating junk food because you have a choice on what you can or cannot eat). Secondly, there has to be a perception of aversive consequences; you need to feel that if you don't resolve the inconsistency, you will pay for it in the future (for example, if you don't stop eating junk food, you feel like you will gain weight and develop lifestyle diseases).

Now that you understand that people are naturally inclined to reduce cognitive dissonance, you can use that fact to persuade people in two different ways: first, you can get then to do something inconsequential, and use that initial behavior to persuade them to do something that's consistent with it. Secondly, you can persuade someone not to do something by logically convincing them that the action is inconsistent with who they are or how they have acted in the past. Thirdly, you can persuade someone to do something by making them realize that the action is consistent with their belief system or other things they have done in the past.

People need to have consistency between their attitudes and their behavior. So, if you want to persuade someone's behavior, you may be able to do it by changing his or her attitude.

Social Judgment Theory

This theory proposes that people make choices based on mediated judgment processes. For a person to be persuaded, he or she has to take in a message, compare that message (and its underlying implications) to his or her current positions on the subject, and then make a decision on whether or not to do what you want him or her to do.

The person's position on the issue at hand often depends on the type of issue: there are cases where the person has a preferred position (a preset conviction); there are other times where the person has to compare several alternatives (these alternatives are known as "latitudes"); finally, there are other cases where the person's ego comes into play, and it affects the decision that he or she makes.

To understand social judgment theory, you have to internalize the concept of latitudes. Latitudes are different levels that reflect a person's attitude towards a certain persuasion attempt. Latitudes are often presented in the form of a spectrum. For example, if a person is trying to get you to do something (e.g. if someone asks you out on a date) the latitudes (attitudinal spectrum) could be: Completely acceptable; Acceptable; Indifferent; Unacceptable; completely unacceptable. In this case, "completely acceptable" and "acceptable" make up the "latitude of acceptance." "Indifferent" makes up the "latitude of non-commitment," "Unacceptable," and "completely non-acceptable" make up the "latitude of rejection."

Your current belief (your "anchor") on the subject of persuasion will fall within one of the latitudes that we have mentioned. For example, if someone is trying to persuade you, and whatever they are asking you falls under the "latitude of acceptance," you are highly likely to comply with their request. If, on the other hand, the message falls squarely within your "latitude of rejection," you are likely to turn the person down.

The "latitudes of non-commitment" (LoN) refers to the areas in the spectrum where you are indifferent. For example, if someone is trying to persuade you on an issue that you have never really thought about, you might not have any "ready to go" views on the matter. The latitude of non-commitment has the least amount of ego-involvement because the person has no opinion on the matter.

In social judgment theory, persuasion occurs in 2 steps. First, there is a judgment; then there is a shift. In the judgment stage, you essentially decide how close the message is to what you believe (where your anchor falls on the matter). In the shifting stage, you decide how to respond to the message (how your anchor will shift after your decision).

Social judgment theory, therefore, dictates that you can only influence someone if their anchor falls within the latitude of acceptance (LoA). However, in practice, you might be able to expand someone's LoA before you try to persuade them of something to increase the chances that they'll accept your request.

To persuade someone, you have to make sure that you present a message that is either within the LoA or the LoN. You can start by presenting a message that is close to the edge of the LoA; this will shift the person's anchor slightly. You can then present subsequent messages that keep shifting the person's anchor and expanding is LoA until you get to a point where the original intended message falls squarely within the latitude of acceptance.

To use social judgment theory to persuade someone, you first have to find out the person's preferred position on the matter. Once you understand his or her position, you might be able to gauge their LoA. You then have to get to work by chipping away at their attitude. For example, if you meet someone that you are attracted to, and you want to be in a relationship with that person; her attitude may range from "willing to date you," all the way to "find you repulsive."

Now, if the person finds you repulsive, she most certainly won't be persuaded to go out on a date with you. However, you can use persuasion techniques to shift her attitude little by little; you can get her from "finds you repulsive" to "willing to tolerate your presence" to "being indifferent about you" to "finding you a bit likable" to "liking you" and so on. The idea is that the shift cannot be drastic because there will be a boomerang effect that reinforces the person's initial attitude towards you.

The Elaboration Likelihood Model

This theory is based on the premise that when people process information, they do it in one of two ways; they either process it cognitively, or they process it superficially. When information is processed cognitively, it goes through the "central route," and the person deeply considers the meaning. If the information is processed superficially, it goes through the "peripheral route."

If your aim is to persuade, you want your target to pay attention to the information you are putting out. This means you want him or her to process the information through the "central route." On the flip side, if you want to sneak some information past a person (if you don't want the person to seriously consider that information) you might want them to process it through the "peripheral route"— companies do this by burying crucial information in the fine print.

There are several factors that determine whether the information will be processed through the central route or through the peripheral route. These factors include: whether the recipient finds the information interesting; whether the information benefits the recipient in some way (self-interest); and whether the information is inherently or universally important (e.g., social issues); whether the recipient has the ability to focus on the information (e.g., their prevailing mood, and the presence of distractions).

If a message is interesting, important, beneficial to the recipient, and delivered when the recipient is focused, then it will be processed through the central route. If the message misses out on one or more of these points, then it might be processed through the peripheral route.

When people process your message through the central route, they will be persuaded by the substance of the message; they'll pay attention to the key points that you are making, to the logical consistency, and to the credibility of your sources. If, however, the message is processed through the peripheral route, your audience will be persuaded by the "form" of your message instead of the substance; they'll focus on things like diction, clarity, your appearance, your level of confidence, or even the immediate environment.

So, if you are looking to persuade someone, you should first try to understand how they are going to process your message. If it's a topic that offers low levels of interest, relevance, importance, or focus, you might want to focus more on the "form" of your presentation rather than the substance because it's highly likely that the person will process the information through the peripheral route.

For example, if you are an architect and you want to persuade a client who doesn't have any knowledge of technical architectural concepts, you might be more effective if you focus on superficial things during your presentation; showcasing your qualifications and awards, creating an aesthetically pleasant models, being articulate during your presentation, etc.

If you are looking to persuade someone on a topic that offers high levels of interest, importance, relevance, focus, and understanding, you might want to focus on the substance because the chances are that the information will be processed through the central route.

For example, if you are an architect interviewing for a job at the best firm in town, you know that you will be dealing with professionals who know their stuff. To persuade them to give you a job, you have to focus on the strength and congruence of your messages, creativity, and originality, the credibility of your sources as well as your own credibility.

CHAPTER 4:

Persuasion Strategies

The ability to persuade others is instrumental to success in almost all walks of life. No matter what career path you take, you will be required, time and again, to convince your coworkers, clients, customers, etc. to do certain things. In your personal life, you will have to persuade your family members, your friends, and your partner to see something from your point of view almost every single day. Persuasion is of the most universally applicable social skills that one can have. To help you be more persuasive, let's discuss the 6 main persuasion strategies.

Reciprocity

The first persuasion strategy is reciprocity. We all have the principle of reciprocity hard-wired into our psychological makeup. When someone does you a favor, you will feel a strong urge to return that favor in one way or another. In fact, reciprocity is thought to be one of the foundational traits that make us social beings.

To use reciprocity as a persuasion strategy, you have to perform a small favor for the person you are trying to persuade, then ask that person for what you wanted all along. A simple example of reciprocity is where you cover for a coworker, and then you ask him or her to help you out with a project. He or she will feel obligated to do what you want. You have to be careful about using this technique with certain people, especially those who have narcissistic tendencies. Such people may feel entitled to your help, so they won't feel any obligation to return the favor.

Another way to use reciprocity to persuade people is by promising to do something for someone and then asking for a favor. If there is trust between two parties (you and the person you are trying to influence), there is a tenancy to take the other person on his or her word. So, if you promise to do something for someone, and the person is convinced that you will keep your word, he will immediately feel the need to reciprocate for that action, even though you are yet to perform it.

For example, you can promise to cover for your coworker in the future, and then ask him or her to help you with your project at the present moment.

When using reciprocity for persuasion, your aim is to offer small favors and get big returns for those favors (otherwise, the technique won't have any utility for you). However, as you do this, you have to remember that people are unlikely to reciprocate when they feel that they are being shortchanged. Avoid using this technique to exploit people; instead, use it to persuade people to do things that also benefit them in some way.

Consistency

The consistency strategy is pretty straightforward, and we already talked about it to some extent when we discussed persuasion theories. As we mentioned, people like to think, feel, and act in a manner that is consistent with their past behavior. This means that when you get people to take certain small actions, they become committed to that kind of behavior, and with time, you might be able to persuade them to take bigger actions in a similar vein.

When someone publicly states his or her goals or makes certain promises to you in the presence of witnesses, it becomes exponentially difficult for him or her to fail to meet that promise because the person is trying to avoid cognitive dissonance and to manage other people's perceptions of him or her.

You can use consistency to persuade someone in a number of different ways. For example, if you want to donate money to save an animal shelter, you may start by asking the person to sign a petition to save the shelter, and then coming back a few days later with the request for money. Once the person signs the petition, he becomes invested in your cause, and he is more likely to donate money at a later date because he feels the need to be consistent.

You can also use consistency to persuade someone during a conversation, by pointing out the things that he has done in the past that are similar to what you want him to do. For example, you can tell a friend that "I have always been able to count on you, and I appreciate it – I need your help again." In this case, your friend is more likely to come through because of the consistency principle.

Social Proof

This persuasion strategy is based on the psychological (and anthropological) fact that when people don't have full information, they make decisions based on other people's decisions. This is a natural tendency that exists everywhere in the animal kingdom, not just in humans. When we live in a society, we don't always have the time or the knowledge to make our own decision, so, as a survival mechanism, we look at what other people are doing, and we do the same thing.

We use social proof to make decisions because we believe that there is strength in numbers. If you are presented with two products that you have never used before, and someone tells you that 80 percent of people prefer product A while only 20 percent of people prefer product B, you will immediately assume that product A is better than product B, and if you have to make a quick decision, you will go with product A because it's the "safe choice" (if all the other factors are constant).

You can use social proof to persuade someone in many different ways. You can convince your friend to attend a party by telling her that all her other friends are going to be there. A waiter can convince a customer to order a certain menu item by saying, "all our really seem to enjoy this week's special." You can convince someone to buy your toothpaste by claiming on your advert that it's recommended by the majority of dentists.

Liking

This persuasion strategy based on a simple concept: people are more easily persuaded by the people they like. You are more likely to perform a favor for your friend that you are to do the same for a total stranger.

The question then becomes; how do you get someone to like you? Studies show that we like people that are similar to us, and we like people who we admire. In other words, we like people because we see ourselves in them, or we like people because we want to be like them.

You can get the person you are trying to persuade to like you first by presenting yourself in a way that makes him believe that you have certain things in common. For instance, you can try to mirror his behavior, or you can identify common interests that the two of you may have, and then have a discussion on those topics.

Getting someone to like you also involves building trust. Try spending time with the person, establishing a rapport with him, and sharing a few experiences before you try to persuade him to do something.

Authority

We covered the importance of coming across as authoritative when we talked about the concept of ethos. The bottom line is that we are all wired to respect authority, whether that authority, is real or perceived. So, we are more likely to be persuaded by someone who seems to be in a position of authority, and you are more likely to listen to someone who appears to be an expert in a certain subject matter. Studies show that patients are more likely to follow their doctors' instructions if the doctors hang copies of their diplomas where the patients can see when they come in for consultations.

To use this technique, all you have to do is present yourself as authoritatively as possible: for example, if you are an entrepreneur pitching to investors, dress as formally as you can, and make sure your presentation is well polished.

Scarcity

Psychologists have long understood that we tend to fear losing out on something or being left out. When we feel that we are about to lose a certain opportunity, we develop a heightened sense of urgency, and we act immediately.

Scarcity can be used as a persuasion strategy in all areas of life. You can get your partner to fall in love with you (or to value your relationship a lot more) by making yourself less available to him. If you are around him all the time, he might take you for granted, but if you always seem to be busy working on something else, he is more likely to pursue you and take your relationship seriously.

Scarcity is mostly used in sales and marketing. For example, real estate agents sell lots of property by convincing their clients that the houses are about to be sold to other clients. Auction sites sell items by placing time limits on bids. Stores move merchandise by pretending to be running out of stock all the time.

CHAPTER 5:

Why You Should Develop Effective Communication Skills

The importance of effective communication skills cannot be overstated. Without communication skills, you cannot fully understand others, and others cannot fully understand you. This essentially means that you will be unable to function optionally, and you are less likely to achieve your goals. Psychologists have done lots of studies on the importance of effective communication skills, and in this chapter, we will look at a brief breakdown of the findings of some of those studies.

Researchers have found that better communicators tend to have better marriages. There are many reasons why marriages fail; marital infidelity and financial problems rank highly on the list, but the failure to communicate is the root of many issues. When there is poor communication in a marriage (or any relationship for that matter), it often means that one person is putting up with a decision he or she doesn't fully agree with. This breeds resentment, and often, the marriage becomes toxic as a result. Effective communication, on the other hand, increases intimacy.

Studies have also found that effective communicators make more money than people with poor communication skills. In career and business situations, people with good communication skills tend to speak up, and their ideas are always heard. As a result, they are perceived as more confident, more competent, and better suited for management positions. They are promoted ahead of their peers, and they ascend the career ladder much faster.

People with effective communication skills tend to have high self-esteem. Such people are more likely to talk to strangers, to be assertive when they feel like they are being shortchanged, and to form quick friendships and adapt to a new environment. As a result, other people tend to perceive them more positively, and they are therefore awarded for their good communication skills; which serves to boost their self-esteem further.

Studies also indicate that effective communication is one of the most important skills that an entrepreneur can have. If you intend to start your own business, you have to sell your idea to all kinds of people: investors, employees, customers, clients, etc. An entrepreneur with a good idea and poor communication skills may fail to articulate his or her ideas during pitch meetings, and this could doom the business from the start.

Effective communication is one of the most sought-after leadership skills. You cannot lead without communicating. As a leader, your team counts on you for direction and motivation. You need to be able to layout your vision in a clear manner. You need to establish communication channels to ensure optimal teamwork. All of these things will be difficult to handle if you have poor communication skills.

The ability to communicate effectively offers you the tools that you need to participate in society. If you want to be a pillar of your community, an active member of the PTA, a local representative, etc. you have to be good at communicating your ideas.

CHAPTER 6:

How Communication and Rhetoric Skills Can Help Persuade People

Communication and rhetoric skills are crucial when it comes to persuasion. After reading thus far, you may have noticed that persuasion has little to do with what you want and more to do with how you ask for it. That's where communication and rhetoric skills come in. whether in your personal life or in your career, rhetoric and communication skills can go a long way in helping you get what you want out of people.

To use your communication skills to persuade people, you first have to know your audience. This is the cardinal rule of communication and persuasion alike. Effective communication is about assessing the needs of the audience. To do that, you need to know the values and the desires of your audience. If your goal is persuasion, chances are you have a fairly narrow audience, and in many cases, you might just be dealing with one individual. In such cases, getting to know your audience shouldn't be that difficult.

If you are looking to persuade a large group of people, it might be enough to understand their general demographic information as you seek to figure out how to communicate with them (for example, you might profile them according to their gender, education background, socio-economic status, etc.) but if you are dealing with one person or a handful of people, it might be imperative for you to dig much deeper.

These days, there's a lot that you can learn about a person from their online and social media profiles. For example, if you are interviewing for a job, you could find out who the panelists are going to be, and you can check both their professional and their personal online profiles.

The point of this is to discover what's important to your audience, and how receptive they are to various communication techniques.

When you get around to conversing with your target audience, you have to ensure that you communicate efficiently. That means using your words in a precise manner. This is a crucial communication technique that is taught to elite salespeople, whose primary job is to persuade people to make purchases. Sales experts are trained to KISS (keep it short and simple) and not to KILL (keep it long and Lengthy).

To communicate efficiently, you have to put out all the important points that you are trying to make in the shortest time possible and close the deal as fast as you can, instead of telling a winding story that dilute your points so that your audience is unaware of what you are trying to pass across.

To converse in an efficient manner, you have to get rid of filler words and phrases such as "I guess," "You know," "Well" and "Uhm." These words not only dilute your points, but they also make you come across as less confident. If you are trying to persuade someone to do something, they will make their decision based on whether they think you are sure of yourself.

Precise speech is a sign of confidence, but it also sounds more sophisticated and more professional. Precision is associated with authority. For example, your doctor won't say, "I guess you can take 2 pills every morning." She will say, "Take 2 pills every morning." The first phrase sounds like a suggestion, and the second one sounds like an order, so as a patient, you will ascribe authority to the second statement and not the first one.

When you speak with the goal of persuading someone, you should use pauses instead of filler words. Pauses are extremely powerful communication tools because they have a way of emphasizing what you've just said. If you speak consciously without pauses, the person you are talking to is more likely to process the information you are relaying in a superficial manner because he or she doesn't have the time to really think about what you are saying. Pauses, however, allow time for the information to sink in, so if you have crafted a well-thought-out argument, your chances of actually persuading your target can increase exponentially.

The use of statements in place of questions is a highly effective rhetoric tool that's used in persuasion. When you are trying to build a rapport with someone before you persuade them, you can use "cold read statements" to get them to engage with you. This is where, instead of asking someone a question, you make a statement about them (based on your observations), and you then get them to react to the statement.

For example, instead of asking someone, "Do you like to have fun?" you can say, "I bet you like to have fun." If you keep asking questions, your target can feel like he or she is on the spot, and he or she can easily shut down. However, if you make cold-read statements, your target will respond and engage with you openly, and you will have an easier time building a rapport with him.

Remember that when you want to persuade someone, the most important thing to that person is how he or she stands to benefit from whatever it is you are asking him to do. So, focus much of the conversation on what they are getting, not what you are getting. If you are trying to sell an idea to a person, you want to be able to create a sense of ownership over that idea in that person. You can do that by using "you" or "we" instead of "I."

Body language is also a crucial part of effective communication. It said that much of our communication is non-verbal, so pay attention to how you position your body, how you use your arms and the kinds of facial expressions that you make when you are talking to the person you want to persuade. You want to come across as open and confident, so avoid a posture that makes you look closed off (e.g., crossing your arms in front of your torso). You also want to display positive facial expressions (e.g., a genuine smile) instead of expressions that indicate negative or indifferent emotions.

CHAPTER 7:

The Dark Triad and How to Develop the Qualities of a Manipulator for Success

Psychologists use the term dark triad to refer to the 3 main negative personality traits that humans possess. These traits are Narcissism, Machiavellianism, and psychopathy. These traits are generally thought to be negative, but there is a lot of evidence out there that shows that they can be useful in helping people to successes in certain areas of life. In this chapter, we will look at the dark triad traits, and we will discuss how these traits can help you manipulate others, in order to succeed, both in your personal life and in your career.

Narcissism

Narcissism it the trait that characterizes narcissist. Narcissists are people who have a heightened sense of entitlement, and they tend to have a sense of superiority and grandiosity. These people believe that they are better than everyone else, and they are always on a mission to dominate the people in their lives. They have big egos, and they often try to control others or to harm them in order to feel their "narcissistic supply." One of their main characteristics is that they have no empathy towards the plight of the people they victimize, and they seem to believe that their feelings and needs matter more than anyone else's.

Narcissists tend to be very particular about how they manipulate or victimize others. First, they always come across as charming and confident. When a narcissist targets you for the purposes of manipulation, he will charm you into trusting him and letting him in.

Narcissists are extremely good at starting relationships with people, they are outgoing, and so they easily connect with strangers. They also use techniques such as seduction and flattery to get people to enter into relationships with them or to let them into their lives. When a narcissist pursues you, he will make you feel like you are the center of his world, and this will blind you to the fact that the narcissist is seducing you because he wants you to let your guard down.

Once a narcissist has earned your trust, he will reveal his true colors to you; and it will be too late. At this point, you would already be emotionally invested in your relationship with him.

Additionally, he would have gathered enough information about you to gain control over your life through things like blackmail, shaming, guilt-tripping, etc.

The thing to note about narcissists is that inasmuch as they appear to have high self-esteem; that is rarely ever the case. Narcissists want to be seen as superior to others, even when they logically understand that they are not. As a result, they become obsessed with controlling how others perceive them. For instance, a narcissist who wants to be seen as smart will go out of his way to force others around him to acknowledge that fact.

Narcissists often react negatively when their curated self-image is not acknowledged by others. For example, if you don't acknowledge how smart he is, the narcissist may try to use insidious techniques to prove that he is indeed smart, and this can create negative consequences for you. Some narcissists may even go so far as to use violence and other coercive techniques to control your perception of them.

What's interesting about narcissist though, is the fact that they are more likely to succeed compared to the average person. As we've mentioned, narcissists have a grandiose view of themselves, and in our society, such views can turn out to be self-fulfilling prophecies. For example, if a narcissist believes that he is smarter than others, he is going to share his ideas during meetings, praise himself in the company of others, and act as if he knows more than everyone else. In other words, he will do everything in his power to prove that he is smarter, and in doing so, he will outwork everyone else and turn out to be the best in his team.

In as much as narcissism is thought to be negative, it can be an indicator of success. This means that if you adopt narcissistic traits (e.g., being manipulative), you can end up succeeding as a direct result of those traits.

Machiavellianism

This is the dark trait that involves trickery and deceitfulness. It is a very complex trait; it's often the dominant trait in the kinds of people who run intellectually-involving manipulation schemes (e.g., white-collar criminals, corrupt politicians, etc.). Machiavellians tend to be highly intelligent people who are cynical about the world. They believe that in their pursuit of success, the end always justifies the means.

The main characteristic of Machiavellians is that they are not limited by conventional morality. While most members of society will stop short of harming others in order to get what they want, Machiavellians have no problem doing so. To them, people are just chess pieces that they have to move around the board if they want to succeed. For all intents and purposes, Machiavellians are a-moral. They have absolutely no sense of right and wrong, and they have an extremely utilitarian view of the world. They always act out of self-interest, and they won't hesitate to hurt you to get what they want.

Machiavellians tend to make decisions in a cold and calculated manner. They don't have principles such as compassion, and they don't have empathy. They'll pursue success by any means necessary. To them, life is a zero-sum game, so they can rationalize any action that causes harm to others. When a Machiavellian takes your side, it's only because your interests are temporarily aligned, and your alliance is beneficial to him. Should your interests diverge in the future, he won't hesitate to treat you as an enemy.

Machiavellians don't seem to have any emotional attachments, and they are not sentimental in any way. That being said, they are very good at understanding how others feel. They have what psychologists refer to as "cold empathy." When someone has cold empathy, it means that he can observe your behavior and predict your emotional reactions, but he won't feel that human connection with you. It means that his empathy is limited to understanding emotions, and it doesn't include putting himself in your shoes and treating you as he would want to be treated.

Machiavellians masters of manipulation and they tend to thrive as both political and business leaders. They can come up with complex machinations that span years, and they can execute those plans while holding their cards close to their chests. That's why it's so difficult to tell if you are dealing with a Machiavellian. He will never reveal his true intentions to you until it's too late.

Machiavellianism can help you succeed in many competitive fields; although it's a dark trait, having it can help you climb the career ladder, or it can even help you become an effective tactician and leader.

Psychopathy

This is by far the most malevolent of the three dark traits. The first thing you need to know about psychopaths is that they totally lack empathy towards others because they lack a conscience. Narcissists can show empathy towards their friends and family, and Machiavellians can use "cold empathy" to understand other people's feelings, but to psychopaths, empathy is an entirely foreign concept.

Psychopaths tend to be very impulsive, and they'd do anything to amuse themselves, including causing serious harm to other people, or performing activities that are highly risky or even violent. They are extremely callous towards others, and they have a grandiose self-image.

It's easy to assume that psychopaths are "crazy" people who are distinct from other members of society, but that's not the case. It's very difficult to spot a psychopath because they appear normal by all indications. They are able to fit into society by copying other people's emotions and feigning empathy.

Since they can fake emotions, psychopaths can be charming or even seductive. They'll manipulate people to get what they want, both in their personal and professional lives. However, they tend to be very volatile, and if they are set off, they can harm someone without compassion.

Psychopathy can be an indicator of success in careers and businesses where total disregard for other people's welfare can be profitable. However, its, for the most part, a negative trait. Psychopathy is an inborn trait, although it can be exacerbated by environmental factors (such as one's upbringing).

Developing the Qualities of a Manipulator for the Purposes of Success

As you can see, the dark traits of manipulative people can be indicators of success, especially in highly competitive careers. There are people who are naturally born with those traits, and they have an unfair advantage over those who don't have these traits. SO, to stay competitive, you might need to learn certain traits of manipulators on your own so that you can apply them and increase your chances of succeeding, not just in your career, but also in your personal life.

You can learn manipulation the same way you learn any other skills; through practice. There are many ways to practice manipulation. First, since manipulation involves a lot of depiction, you might want to take acting lessons so that you can practice expressing emotions that you aren't really feeling at the moment.

Almost every manipulation technique out there involves telling a lie, and any lie you tell can quickly unravel if your delivery isn't convincing enough. The thing to remember here is that people can naturally sense that you are lying if your body language is not consistent with what you are saying. Acting can help you express emotions that come across as genuine. So, you can become better at deception just by taking acting lessons at a theatre near you (these days, it's even possible to take such lessons online).

You can also practice manipulation by practicing public speaking or participating in debates. The effectiveness of your manipulation techniques has a lot to do with how well you are able to communicate with confidence. When you manipulate people, they are more likely to believe you if you deliver your ideas in a coherent and structured way.

One key quality of an effective manipulator lies in his ability to establish similarities with the person he is targeting in order to get that person to connect with him. There are many ways to establish similarity. One such method involves "mirroring." This is a manipulation technique where you imitate the other person's behavior in order to build a rapport with him, and in order to make him more receptive to your ideas. you can try to copy the other person's posture, the placement of their arms, or even their facial expressions; remember to do this as subtly as you can to avoid making him self-conscious.

To be an effective manipulator, you have to come across as charismatic. It's no accident that charismatic people always seem to get what they want: when a person comes across as charming, confident, and collected, people tend to immediately trust him, and they let their guard down when he is around.

When you are charismatic, you make other people feel special. Charisma comes naturally to some people, but you can learn it through practice. You can pay attention to the people you are interacting with (through eye contact and by practicing active listening). This will show them that you really care about them, and they'll feel secure enough to let you in. as a result, your manipulation technique will be a lot more effective.

Finally, manipulation is mostly about taking advantage of others' weaknesses. To learn people's weakness, you need to know how to read them. You can practice reading people by closely watching their body language and paying attention to their verbal cues. Take the time to figure out whether the person you are targeting is susceptible to emotional responses, or if he is more inclined to process information in a rational way. This will go a long way in helping you select an effective manipulation technique to use against the person.

CHAPTER 8:

What Is Emotional Intelligence (EI)?

Emotional intelligence is defined as a person's ability to recognize and correctly identify his or her own emotions, as well as the emotions of others with who he or she interacts.

Emotional intelligence generally has 2 parts to it, first, it's the ability to discern one's own feelings, to accurately label those feelings, and to use that information, as well as an understanding of oneself to guide one's own behavior and thinking, in order to regulate one's emotions, to adapt to one's social environment, and to succeed in one's goals.

Secondly, it's the ability to observe other people's actions, reactions, behavior, etc. in order to understand their emotions, so as to predict the way they would react under specific circumstances; this ability gives the person who possesses it an upper hand when it comes to influencing others and getting what he or she wants out of social interactions.

Emotional Intelligence is an extremely important indicator of success in many areas of life. People with higher emotional intelligence tend to enjoy better mental health because they are better emotionally adjusted than their counterparts with lower emotional intelligence. Emotional intelligence also predicts job performance in many careers, especially those that deal with lots of interpersonal interactions (e.g., sales and marketing). Emotionally intelligent people are also known to have better leadership skills because, for the most part, leadership is about being able to understand the emotional needs of others, and being able to communicate with them in an effective way.

Scholars like to compare emotional intelligence (also known as emotional quotient and abbreviated as EQ) to general intelligence (IQ). These two forms of intelligence are very different from each other. IQ has been part of the general metric for intelligence for a long time, and rudimentary IQ tests date back to ancient China. EQ, on the other hand, is a fairly new concept. It's first started appearing in psychological literature back in the 1960s, but it wasn't until the 1990s that author Daniel Goleman articulated the concept, and defined it in the conventional way that we understand it today.

One core difference between IQ and EQ is that IQ is something that you are born with, and it remains fairly constant throughout one's life, while EQ is something that you learn during your developmental stages, and it is technically a skill that you can sharpen with concerted effort. This means that where IQ is concerned, you are stuck with your natural ability, but where EQ is concerned, it's within your ability to apply yourself and to improve.

SO, is EQ more important than IQ when it comes to predicting success? Well, that is a fairly complex question. IQ is definitely an important metric when it comes to predicting a person's ability to perform complex tasks, but EQ may be a better indicator of success than IQ in some instances.

For example, if it takes an IQ of 125 to be a good entrepreneur, a person with an IQ of 130 might be able to outperform a person with an IQ of 135 if he is more emotionally adjusted (i.e., if he has a higher EQ) than his "traditionally smarter" counterpart. So, if you want to increase your chances of success in whatever you are pursuing, don't waste your time worrying about your IQ because it's something you might not be able to change. Instead, focus on improving your EQ, because you can absolutely change it.

CHAPTER 9:

Essential Abilities of an Emotionally Intelligent Person

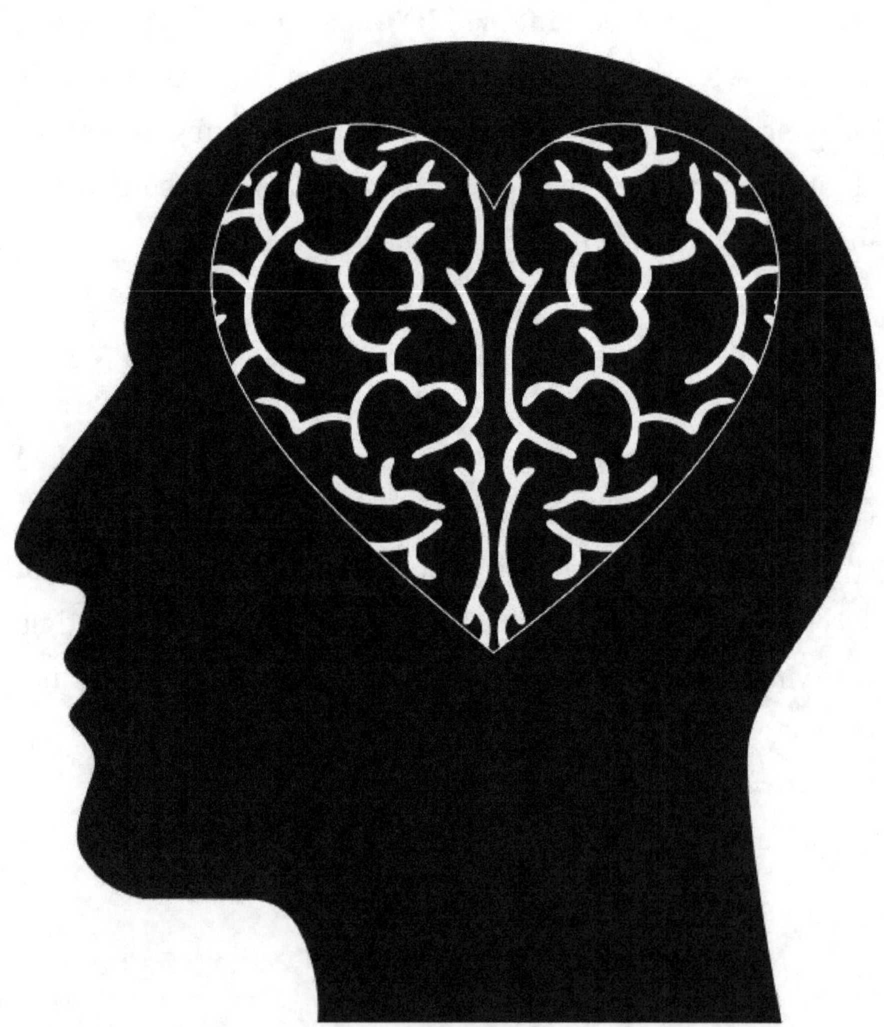

When Goleman pioneered the concept of emotional intelligence as we understand it today, he came identified five features of emotional intelligence. These, according to him, were the five abilities that a person needs to have in order to be considered emotionally intelligent. These abilities are self-awareness, self-regulation, empathy, motivation, and social skills. In this chapter, we will take a look at each of those abilities, and we will discuss how you can develop each one of them.

Self-Awareness

According to Goleman, self-awareness is the ability of a person to accurately recognize his or her own emotions, his or her own strengths, and weaknesses, and to be conscious of his or her own actions, and how all those things affect other people around him or her.

Self-awareness has several benefits to the individual. First, increases the chances that one will be able to handle constructive criticism. When you are self-aware, you will be able to set your ego aside when someone criticizes you, and you will be able to draw lessons from what others say about you without taking things personally. In the same vein, when you have self-awareness, you will be able to criticize others without making them feel like you are initiating personal attacks against them.

In a sense, self-awareness is about being in touch with how you feel. When you are self away, you process emotions a lot better, and you are therefore more likely to have mature relationships with the people in your life.

The other component of self-awareness, as we have mentioned, is about understanding your strengths and weaknesses, and that can go a long way in helping you succeed in life. For example, if you are running a business, and you discover that you have certain weaknesses, you can increase your chances of succeeding by hiring someone who can perform well in areas where you struggle. If you are starting a relationship, you can find a partner whose strengths complement yours.

To improve your self-awareness, you need to keep a record of situations where you are emotionally triggered so that you can analyze them and identify any issues that you may have. Once you decide to pursue emotional awareness, start keeping a diary or a journal.

When you experience negative emotions such as anger, or even when you experience strong positive emotions, you should note down the incident in as much detail as possible. Write down what emotion you experienced, how intense the emotion was, what you believe triggered the emotion, how long it lasted, etc. After keeping a record for a few days or even weeks, you can sit down and review the record in order to identify any connections between different incidences.

Where our emotions are concerned, we all have certain blind spots. That's why it's important to seek the help of others as you try to increase your self-awareness. Ask the people close to you, the ones you trust, to be honest, to tell you what they think your strengths and weaknesses are. It's very easy to overlook your own weaknesses, and it's almost just as easy to underestimate your own strengths, so an objective observer can be very helpful when it comes to figuring things out.

You should also try to take notice of how specific people around you affect your behavior. People can indeed influence your behavior without you realizing it. You might find that you are happy around certain people, and you are uncomfortable around certain other people. Taking stock of these tendencies can help you understand and improve your relationship with other people.

Self-Regulation

Self-regulation is the quality that allows an individual to manage his or her own emotional impulses so that he or she can be more effective in asserting for himself or herself during social discourse and being more in control of his or her actions to increase productivity and his or her chances of success. Self-regulation is quite simply about controlling your own emotions. It's about retraining yourself despite the urge to react in an emotional way. It's about putting and instead, reacting to a situation in a way that is beneficial to you, and to other parties.

For instance, if your coworker or even you child does something wrong, and you feel angry, your instinct may be to lash out and to shout at him or her, but self-regulation allows you to see the bigger picture; that it's better for everyone if you stay collected, calmly express your disapproval, and tell them how to fix the problem.

One of the main benefits of self-regulation is that it helps you to retain control over any situation by retaining the trust and respect of the person that you are interacting with. If you react with negative emotion in any social interaction, you immediately lose something; reason goes out the window, and you go off-track. However, if you regulate your emotions, you are more likely to stay the course and to have an adult conversation with the other person.

Self-regulation helps you to adapt to changes. If you can self-regulate, there is nothing that can throw you off balance. You will be able to make any changes in stride without feeling overwhelmed or too anxious. Emotions can be paralyzing, so self-regulation is just what you need to be able to move forward in the face of challenges.

More importantly, self-regulation allows you to react in a rational way, no matter the situation. When emotions take over, we become less rational, and we end up making poor decisions. If you have self-regulation, you will still experience emotions, but you will be able to manage them in an instance, and your rational brain will immediately resume control over your thinking process, so your decision-making skills won't be impaired.

If you want to increase your self-regulation, you can do so by practicing taking responsibility for everything that happens to you. Even if something that has happened is clearly someone else's fault, it doesn't mean that you cannot take responsibility. So, if someone screws up and it affects you, remind yourself that quickly resolving the problem is better than lashing out with anger, or any other negative emotion.

You can also learn self-regulation by taking a deep breath before you react when you experience negative emotions. Once you feel a surge of emotions coming in, just breathe in, hold it for a few seconds, and breathe out, before you react. This simple exercise can help you regulate yourself, and it can keep you from escalating emotional situations.

Social Skills

There are many things that can fall under the category of social skills; anything that can help you coexist with other people can technically be considered to be a social skill. The most common social skills include assertiveness, communication skills, accepting and delivering constructive criticism, teamwork, effective listening, the ability to "agree to disagree," handling peer pressure, and most importantly, conflict resolution.

Good social skills can help you build a rapport with anyone you meet, and they can help you get along with all other fair-minded people. These skills help you get along with your family members, sustain friendships that are mutually beneficial, and work well with your colleagues.

Social skills are universally applicable. This means that when you develop social skills, you can apply them anywhere, and they can make you an all-round better person.

To develop social skills, you have to practice each individual skill as frequently as you can. You also have to subject yourself to challenging social situations so that you learn how to deal with people and social pressure.

Empathy

As we've mentioned, empathy is the ability to identify and to relate with other people's feelings. It's the ability to see things from someone else's point of view. When you have empathy, you are able to understand how someone else feels, and you can, therefore, treat that person with compassion. Empathy is important because it helps you get along with others, and that matters greatly in almost every aspect of life. Empathy makes you better at everything: it makes you a better friend, a better leader, a better parent, and a better partner.

Empathy indicates to the other person that you care about him or her. For this reason, empathy can help strengthen pretty much any kind of relationship.

To develop empathy, the first thing you need to do is just imagine yourself in other people's positions. When someone talks about his or her experiences, even if you have never been in a similar situation, just use your imagination and picture yourself going through the same thing. Ask yourself, "How would that have felt if it happened to me?"

You can also practice active listening to increase your empathy. Most people don't really listen when others are talking. In most cases, they keep thinking about what they are going to say next when it's their turn to speak. Try to avoid doing this, and just pay attention to what the other person says. You should also avoid interrupting people when they are talking.

When you notice that people seem emotionally distressed, try to offer them some support. For instance, if you see that a friend is worried or he seems distant, you can tell him to feel free to share whatever's on his mind with you. Empathy is not necessarily about solving someone's problems. Sometimes, it's just about letting the person know that they have your support.

As you develop empathy, try to understand people instead of judging them. Our minds are designed to make quick judgments about people and situations, but you should try to push back against that inclination, and gather more information instead of jumping to conclusions. When someone acts a certain way, try to figure out why he does so, instead of just settling on the first explanation that pops into your mind.

You also have to be able to communicate your empathy. When you empathize with someone, show it to them. Use your tone of voice and your body language to indicate to the person that you get where he is coming from, and you understand how he feels.

Motivation

When you are self-motivated, it means that you like what you do, and you aver clear goals that you are working towards. It means that you do what you do because you find it inherently enjoyable, and not because it brings you money or social status.

There are very many advantages of self-motivation. For starters, if you are motivated, you are less likely to procrastinate and to waste your time, so you will be more productive in whatever you do. Self-motivated people tend to perform better at work, at school, and even within relationships.

Motivation also increases your self-confidence. When you are motivated, you believe in yourself, and your ability to work hard and to accomplish your goals. This means that you will be able to advance in your career, to build wealth, and even to inspire other people around you. Motivation can be infectious; if you are motivated, you can spread it around the other people who need it.

The other advantage of motivation is that it increases your chances of overcoming setbacks. People who lack motivation tend to give up at first sight of resistance, but motivated people can overcome the most difficult challenges and press on towards their goals even when no one else believes in them.

Motivation helps you focus on accomplishing your goals, and it reduces the temptation to give up, change your goals, or to get distracted and end up following other people's goals instead of your own.

In order to increase your motivation, you need to set clear goals for yourself. Take some time to figure out what you really want out of life and write down your goals and mission in a clear and precise statement. When you know your life's purpose, you will be more motivated to work towards it.

Make sure that the goals you pursue are in line with the values that are most important to you. If your goals contradict your core values and your passions, you will find it really difficult to stay motivated for a long time.

CHAPTER 10:

How Human Behavior Is Influenced by Emotion

Our emotions clearly influence the way we behave; when you feel happy, you smile. When you are unhappy, you frown. When you are disgusted, you smear. These reactions are so simple and so obvious that we never really stop to wonder how they come about.

Your body and your mind are intricately wired together so that your behavior is a reflection of your state of mind. In fact, some of our behavioral responses to emotions tend to be involuntary. This means that whether you like it or not, your emotions have a say on your behavior.

When any emotion is triggered in your brain, the message is passed on to your nervous system, and a physiological reaction occurs in your body; one that you cannot control. The involuntary reaction that you experience increases the chances that you will make certain voluntary actions; for example, if someone startles you, and you experience fear, your heart will race, and this will increase the chances that you will jump or run away. Similarly, if you are angry, the physiological reaction that comes with the anger increases the chances that you will lash out at someone.

If you behave in a certain way in response to a certain emotion, and you want to change that behavior, it would be futile for you to try and change the underlying emotion. Emotions have evolved over thousands of years to help us survive and coexist, so they are hard to shake. Instead of seeking to change an emotion, try to manage your behavioral response to it.

For example, if you tend to lash out and get into screaming matches when you are angry, don't focus on putting an end to the anger. Instead, focus on changing what you do in response to the anger. You can be able to channel any "negative" emotion into positive behavior. An emotion like anger can be channeled into motivation. An emotion like anxiety can be channeled into focus.

Part of emotional intelligence if figuring out how you can use your emotions to induce constructive behavior rather than destructive ones. From now on, it may be beneficial for you to think of your emotions, not as something that you have to suppress, but something on which you might be able to capitalize. Think of every emotion as a tool, and ask yourself, "How can I channel it to help me achieve my goals?"

CHAPTER 11:

Read People's Emotions Using Your EI

Reading people's emotions is much easier than it sounds. The fact is that you experience emotions that are similar to those of other people, so, even without formal training, you might be able to identify some of the most common expressions.

Reading emotions involves understanding their cues. Where emotions are concerned, verbal cues alone can be misleading, so you need to pay attention to both verbal and nonverbal cues and try to find consistency across different cue clusters in order to correctly identify the emotion in question.

Reading Verbal Cues

You can learn a lot about a person's emotional state based on what he or she says, but you have to remember that words don't reveal everything. Sure, there are certain words that when used, can indicate if, say, a person is angry, sad, etc., but people are pretty good at lying to conceal their true feelings.

Where verbal cues are concerned, you should pay attention to the person's tone of voice. Often times, emotions are revealed, not by what someone says, but how he or she says it. A soft tone can indicate worry or sadness. A sarcastic tone can indicate contempt or even anger. Tone often reveals the speaker's attitude, and attitude always leads back to the underlying emotion.

Other than the tone of voice, the person's pitch can also reveal what he or she is feeling at the moment. The term pitch refers to the highness or lowness of the voice. A high pitch indicates strong emotions, and low pitch often indicates boredom or indifference.

The use of pauses during speech can also reveal something about the speaker's emotional state. If the speaker is nervous, he may speak fast, without pauses in between sentences. If he is relaxed or serious, he may use pauses to stress the point he is making.

Reading Non-Verbal Cues

Facial expressions are perhaps the most revealing indicators of a person's emotional state. What's more, facial expressions tend to be universal: no matter where you go in this world, a smile will indicate happiness, and a frown will indicate sadness. The issue with facial expressions is that sometimes, people can try to fake them in order to mislead anyone that might be trying to figure out how they are feeling. However, even when people fake their facial expression, you may still be able to observe their micro-expressions.

Micro expression a brief flashing facial expression that cannot be faked; they always reveal the person's true emotions. When people are deceptive, they may put on a fake smile, a fake worried look, etc. to make you think they are feeling a certain way. However, since physiological reactions to emotions tend to be involuntary, there is a lag between the time when a person experiences an emotion, and when he makes a conscious decision to show a fake emotion. In that short window of time, the person will flash a micro expression. If you observe the person keenly, you will be able to spot and identify the micro expression as fast as possible before it's gone.

There are 7 main micro-expressions that you need to be able to identify.

The first microexpression is one of joy. It's the micro expression that people display when they experience happiness. It's characterized by the following cues: the cheeks are slightly raised, the lips are pulled backward, and the corners of the lips go upwards, the mouth is slightly parted, and the teeth are partially exposed. Crow's feet are formed in the outer part of the eye, while the lower eyelids are either tensed or slightly wrinkled.

The joy microexpression is important because it can help you distinguish between a real smile and a fake one. A real smile reaches the eyes (crow's feet form on the sides) while a fake smile only involves the lips and cheeks.

The second microexpression is the one that indicates surprise. It's indicated by the following facial cues: the eyelids are opened as wide as possible, and the white part of the eye is visible on both the upper and the lower ends. The person's forehead is horizontally wrinkled. The jaw opens, and the teeth are parted. The skin on the brow area is stretched on the bottom parts.

The microexpression for sadness involves the following cues: the persons' lower lip forms a pout, the skin below the eyebrows creates a triangle, of which the inner corners for the peak and the jawbone is pulled in an upward direction.

The microexpression for fear has the following signs: the mouth is wide open, but the lips are either tense, or they stretched backward. The white part of the eye is visible on the upper side but not on the lower side. The eyebrows are lifted upward, and they are aligned. The middle part of the forehead is wrinkled.

The microexpression for anger comes with the following cues: the lower jaw is pulled outwards, vertical wrinkles appear in the area between the two brows and extending to the forehead, where the wrinkles for at the center, the lips are pushed together, and they form a square shape, the brows move downwards and inwards, the nostrils are flared, and the eyes bulge out.

The microexpression for contempt is the classic smear: the person raises one corner of his lips upwards, higher than the other corner. This is similar to the microexpression for hate.
The microexpression for disgust has the following cues: the lower lip and the cheeks are raised. The upper eyelids are also raised. Lines may form on the lower eyelids. The nose is furrowed.

Body Language Indicators of Emotion

Apart from facial expression, there are certain gestures, postures, and body movements that can reveal a person's emotions.

When a person is happy, he may assume a posture that indicates that he is comfortable. His muscles may seem relaxed, and his arms and legs may be in an open position.

When a person is surprised, he may move his body backward at the exact moment when the surprise registers in his mind.

When a person is angry, he may clench his fists, his lips may tremble, he may use gestures that seem exaggerated, and he may do what it takes to avoid eye contact with you. In other instances, he may invade your personal space or act aggressively.

When a person is sad, he may take up a "limb" posture, and his lips may quiver, and you might be able to see the sadness in his eyes.

When a person is embarrassed, his cheeks and neck may become flushed (appear redder than usual) because of the increase blood flow to the area, and he may put on a fake smile (on that doesn't reach the eyes).

CHAPTER 12:

Influence People's Behavior Using Your EI

In order to influence people in an emotionally intelligent way, you first have to earn their trust and to learn as much as you can about them before you make your influence attempt. In many cases, you'll need to build a rapport with the person, and you might even have to create a real relationship with him or her over a considerable period of time before they trust you enough to accept your influence. However, sometimes, you might have to influence someone who perceives you as an adversary. In such cases, you might have to use a bit of manipulation to persuade the person to see things your way.

Influencing a person's behavior is about planting ideas in their minds in order to actively guide their actions. To that end, it's best to take a friendly approach instead of an antagonistic one. People are less inclined to accept your influence if you come across as bossy or demanding. So, if you want to get someone to do something for you, you are better off starting by asking him questions that they will quickly answer in the affirmative.

By all means, you should avoid giving orders to the people you are trying to influence. Unless you are his boss, the person you are trying to influence will feel disrespected if you make your request sound like an order, even if you throw in the word "Please." In cases where you want to influence someone to do something, and he has no obligation to comply, you are more likely to get his cooperation if, instead of ordering him to do something, you frame your request as a question, or as a subtle suggestion. For example, instead of telling your roommate, "Do the dishes." You'll be more influential if you ask him "would you mind doing the dishes?"

Flattery is one of the most effective ways to influence people's behavior, and it's applicable in almost every social setting. Flattery is about buttering someone up before asking them for a favor or trying to influence them in another way. You should be very careful in your use of flattery, particularly with adults because the older someone gets, the wiser they become, and they more likely they are to see through a compliment. When using flattery with adults, make it sound as genuine as possible, and not exaggerated at all.

When you know that a certain flattering comment is going to sound a bit embarrassing, you can stringed its effect by acknowledging the fact that it's indeed embarrassing. You can use phrases like "I know you wouldn't want me to say this, but…" before delivery a compliment if you want someone to accept it rather than to feel embarrassed by it. Psychologists have noted that using such a phrase can disguise the flattery, make the compliment sound heartfelt, and it also makes the person receiving the compliment come across as highly modest.

Flattery and compliments also work better when there is an audience present, so if you are trying to influence someone, you might want to compliment them around his or her friends before making a request of them.

Another way to influence people in an emotionally intelligent way is through the use of social pressure. People want to fit in and to be liked by others, so they will feel a greater sense of obligation to comply with a request that you make if you do it in the presence of others, or if you bring social pressure to bear in one way or another.

If you want to influence your friend to do you a favor, you can use social influence techniques such as triangulation to get them to do what you want. Triangulation works in several different ways, but in any case, it involves getting other members of your social circle to do the bidding for you. For example, you can tell a mutual friend to make a request on your behalf. This way, the person you are targeting finds it a bit difficult to turn you down, because there is added pressure for him to comply.

You can also influence people's behavior by boosting their confidence in you so that when you make a request, they comply because they have faith in you. An emotionally intelligent person should be able to inspire confidence in the way he or she speaks. He or she may sound more confident by avoiding using words that indicate doubt and probability, and instead, using words that indicate certainty. For example, instead of using words such as "might" and "try" (and other variations of these words), you could be more influential if you use words like "will."

If you are trying to influence the behavior of a person with whom you have an adversarial relationship, the worst thing you can do is belittle their opinion. If you mock someone's point of view on any matter, their ego and emotions will take control, and you will be unable to reason with them and convince them to change their behavior.

Instead, you should make it sound like you understand where they are coming from, and why a reasonable person might have their point of view instead of yours. Use the other person's positive points; as you converse with the person, compare their set of facts with yours before making the point that their points are strong, but yours are just a little bit stronger. This way, you won't bruise the other person's ego, and he will do what you want because it sounds reasonable to him.

CHAPTER 13:

What Does Cognitive Behavioral Therapy (CBT) Involve?

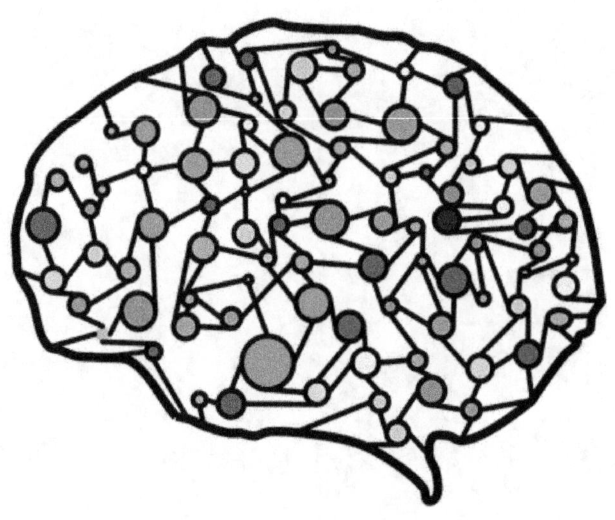

If you have a major mental health issue or even a minor psychological hang-up, you might want the help of a professional therapist. CBT is one of the most common therapy techniques used today to treat all sorts of psychological issues. CBT generally involves two things. It combines the examination of things that you think (cognitive therapy) and the things that you do (behavioral therapy).

Compared to traditional psychotherapy (where you would lie on a couch and talk about how you feel), CBT is a more practical approach to therapy because it involves the use of lots of exercises. CBT is more goal-oriented, and it takes a shorter timespan than psychotherapy. Instead of talking about your feelings, you and your therapist come up with very specific goals that you work towards.

Instead of discussing your dreams, you're past, etc. CBT involves identifying problems that you are experiencing at that very moment and coming up with practical exercises to fix those problems. For example, if you have anxiety, your CBT therapist will focus on treating the anxiety as fast as possible instead of dwelling on digging into your past to find the root cause of the anxiety.

CBT is based on the simple premise that your thoughts affect the way you feel, which in turn affects the way you behave. So, if a thought is triggered, it's going to turn into a feeling and into a subsequent behavior. Here is a simple example of how this cycle works; you find yourself stuck in traffic on your morning commute, you have a bad thought that your boss will be angry if you show up to work late. You feel stressed and anxious as a result. And you start honking at other drivers to get out of the way.

Such patterns of thought and behavior may recur in your life over and over until bye become bad habits. For example, if something goes wrong and you get stressed out, anxious, or you blame yourself, it may start with a few incidences, but the more you follow that pattern, the more you internalize it, and in the end, you will develop low self-esteem.

A CBT therapist will use recent incidents in your life to teach you how to break the negative cycles. The therapist can help you do this in one of two ways; he can help you change your negative thoughts and feelings; he can help you change your negative behavior.

CBT is universally applicable to most psychological and behavioral issues, including dealing with stress, depression, anxiety, eating disorders, substance abuse, sleep issues, or even serious mental conditions such as schizophrenia.

The beauty of CBT is that it can be delivered in many different modalities. It can be used in one on one therapy sessions, in group sessions, through self-help books, through videos, or even over online sessions. This means that you don't necessarily have to book a session with a therapist to make use of CBT. It's something that you can practice on your own through the use of books and free online resources.

CBT has one major limitation; it might not be able to solve deep-rooted issues, and unless it's practiced diligently, it's only going to be a temporary fix.

CHAPTER 14:

What Are CBT Skills?

CBT skills are various techniques that CBT therapists teach their patients to help them deal with mental and psychological issues. For example, if you have anger issues and you consult a CBT practitioner, he will give you certain tools and techniques which you can use whenever you feel angry to manage your emotions by controlling your thoughts and your behavior. CBT skills can be learned by anyone, and as long as you understand how a skill works, you might not need to visit a therapist at all. You can learn CBT skills by reading books or watching videos. In this chapter, we discuss some of the most common, and the most effective CBT skills that can help you deal with a multitude of psychological issues.

Journaling

This is one of the most essential CBT skills that you can learn because it gives you the ability to document and therefore, to understand your own thoughts and moods. When keeping a CBT journal, you will have to write down every time you experience strong emotions, changes in your mood, or negative thoughts, depending on the underlying issue that you are trying to resolve. For instance, if you are dealing with stress, you'll need to document the time when the stress sets in, the thoughts that accompany or trigger the stress, the source of your stress, and even the intensity or the extent of the stress.

In your journal, you have to describe the experiences in as much detail as you can. This will help you figure out if you have certain emotional tendencies, or if you are inclined to have certain thought patterns that lead to negative behavior. By understanding yourself, you are in a better position to adapt, cope, or to change.

Unraveling Your Cognitive Distortions

This is an extremely important basic CBT skill; in fact, it's arguably the primary goal of CBT. We all have our cognitive distortions, but if they lead to negative thoughts and behavior, or if they cause you long term psychological harm, you have to unravel them. Cognitive distortions are those automatic thoughts that pop into your mind when you have certain experiences.

For example, if you make a small mess at work, you are going to worry about getting fired, and you may end up dwelling on that thought too much and blowing things out of proportion. The 'worst-case scenario' mentality is a common cognitive distortion, and it can be very harmful; it causes stress, anxiety, and even depression.

To unravel your cognitive distortions, you have to write down your thoughts or say them out loud, and then go over them with a fine-tooth comb and question every assumption that you are making, and review every logical leap that you are making. This may help realize that your assumptions are misgiven, and that, even if the situation is bad, it's certainly not as apocalyptic as you are inclined to assume.

Let's take the example of someone who is trying to deal with social anxiety. When such a person is invited to a social event, he or she may immediately start worrying about what will happen at the event, and this could lead him or her to turn down the opportunity. This person can unravel his or her cognitive distortions by breaking his or her excuses down and checking to see if they are logical (if, say, the person thinks he will feel out of place at the party, he can challenge that assumption by noting that he knows several other people who will be attending).

Cognitive Restructuring

This CBT skill involves seeking to understand why your cognitive distortions took root in the first place. You have to look back and try to understand why you started believing those things in the first place. Through journaling, you will discover certain patterns in your thoughts and behavior; cognitive restructuring requires you to figure out why you have those thought patterns, and this helps you to challenge them and get rid of them.

Let's say for example, that you have a decent job that pays you well enough to live comfortably, a job that you can do fairly well, but you are stressed out all the time because you think that you need more money. To deal with your stress, you can try to find out why you believe that you need more money to be happy.

You might discover that this idea took root when you were younger, and you had a more fantastical view of the world, so you had unrealistic expectations. Now you have a decent job, but you never really recalibrated your expectations, so you feel like a failure. The other root cause of the problem might be that due to your exposure to pop-culture, you started associating symbols of wealth (such as fancy cars and luxury mansions) with happiness.

In this case, cognitive restructuring will involve redefining what happiness means to you. If you ask yourself "what will make me happy?" you will be able to generate a list of things that you want out of life, and you can then analyze that list and reevaluate the metrics by which you measure happiness.

Other CBT Skills

Apart from the universal CBT skills that we have discussed above, there are hundreds of other CBT skills, most of which are applicable to specific mental or psychological conditions. For example, there are CBT skills that are tailor-made to deal with OCD and other disorders. If you are dealing with a garden-variety issue such as anxiety, stress, or anger, you can learn CBT skills on your own and use them to improve yourself. However, if you are dealing with a serious disorder (one that rises to the level of clinical significance), you might want to consult a trained mental health professional so that he or she can create a special CBT programmer for you.

CHAPTER 15:

Use CBT to Build the Right Mindset

As you've seen so far, you can use CBT to counteract negative thoughts and to build the right mindset. If you experience negative emotions all the time, it doesn't mean that you are incapable of having positive feelings. It just means that you haven't been allowing yourself to experience positive thoughts and feelings. Psychologists call this "dampening"; a process where you unknowingly adopt a negative mindset, and a pessimistic outlook.

Let's look at techniques that you can use to counteract negativity and to create the right mindset.

Finding the Problem and Brainstorming Possible Solutions

We have already looked at how you can use journaling as a technique to identify the pervasive thought patterns that lead to the wrong mindset. Journaling is important because writing things down is the best way to articulate them. If you are feeling pessimistic or negative at the moment, you can try to define, in one clear sentence, what your problem is.

For instance, people who deal with depression often encounter feelings of hopelessness; that's you, try to articulate exactly how you feel at the moment.

After knowing how you feel, you know have to figure out how you want to feel. You can write that down too. So, your current feelings are your starting point, and the way you want to feel is your goal. After establishing those two points, you have to brainstorm ways to move from the first point (e.g., depression) to the final point (e.g., having the right mindset).

Create a list of "action steps" that you can take. They should be easy things that you can do in a moment's notice to significantly change your situation.

The idea here is that instead of focusing on a negative thought and letting it fester, you immediately decide what positive feeling you want to have, and you figure out the little steps that could get you from where you are and where you want to be. If you are stressed about a deadline at work, instead of dwelling on the anxiety that you feel, figure out what steps you need to take to beat that deadline and then take the first step as fast as you can.

Using Self-Statements to Combat Negative Thoughts

You can get yourself into the right mindset by coming up with, writing down, and repeatedly reciting self-statements that counteract your negative thoughts. Whenever the negative thoughts creep into your mind, recite your prepared self-statement several times, until it takes the place of the negative thought.

As a point of caution, avoid coming up with a self-statement that creates cognitive dissonance. For instance, if the prevailing negative thoughts in your head is "imp feeling so anxious right now," don't try to replace it with "I'm feeling confident right now." If you do this, your mind will reject the self-statement, and this might put you in a worse state of mind. Instead, your self-statement can be "everyone feels a bit nervous when they encounter challenging situations." Here, you are not trying to force the anxiety out; you are just trying to regain control over your nerves so that you can think more clearly. So, there is no cognitive dissonance, and your mind will accept your self-statement.

Look for Opportunities to Think Positively

Psychologists have long understood that we are the sum of our experiences. That means that if you have more negative experiences than positive ones, then you will have a negative mindset, but if you have more positive experiences than negative ones, you will develop a positive mindset. So, it's a numbers game.

One CBT technique for developing a positive mindset involves listing the things that you like about something, even if it's a negative thing. For example, if you walk into a room and you immediately decide that you don't like the place, you can train yourself to look around and notice a handful of things about which you feel positively.

You can do this with anything, person, place, or situation. For example, if you dislike your coworker and you find that it affects your job performance, you could try listing five things that you like about him or her. When those five things are at the top of your mind, you might be amazed to find that you have a net-positive mindset towards the person.

Recap the Best Parts of Your Day

The overarching narrative of your life is what determines whether you'll have a positive mindset or a negative one. So, at the end of each day, use the CBT technique that involves visualizing the best parts of the day before you go to sleep. Even if you have had a hectic day, just look back at the day, and try to identify the parts that you really enjoyed. You can write those experiences down in your journal.

As you do this, with time, you will notice that you are looking forward to having a great day. In the mornings, you will start wondering, "what will be the best parts of today?" instead of thinking that it's just going to be another hectic workday.

Accept the Fact That Disappointment Is a Part of Life

The reason we get overwhelmed by negative experiences is that we lend them too much weight. When something goes wrong, we obsess over the situation to the point of paralysis; and the more we obsess, the bigger the problem becomes.

To prevent this, you can use the CBT technique that involves acknowledging the fact that disappointing situations are bound to cross your path, so, when you encounter them, you don't feel overwhelmed. When something goes wrong, allow yourself to feel disappointed, but don't let it consume you.

CHAPTER 16:

What Are Social Skills?

These are skills and techniques that we all use every day during social interactions. They are necessary skills that we need to communicate with each other, and to get what we want out of all kinds of interactions. Social skills cover everything, from verbal and non-verbal communication skills, the ability to read other people's body language, the ability to be sociable, etc.

There are lots of advantages when it comes to having well developed social skills. First and foremost, social skills enable you to have better relationships with every metric. When you have social skills, you will have more friends, personal relationships that are more fulfilling, and a better social support system. People with good social skills tend to be more charismatic, and that is a universally desirable trait. Charismatic people just seem to be inherently more interesting.

Without social skills, it's practically impossible to advance anywhere in life. No matter how smart you are (as an employee) or how good you are (as a friend or a potential romantic partner) you will still find yourself losing out to people who have perfected their social skills. Developing social skills can help you develop pretty much every kind of relationship that you may venture into.

Social skills make you a better communicator, and effective communication is the key to influencing people. Communication skills technically fall under the category of social skills, and in many cases, they are one and the same.

Social skills also make you more efficient and more productive in whatever you do. If you are good with people, you can apply that in and field to make you more effective at what you do. Even if you are inclined to avoid spending time with someone, good social skills enable you to let that person down gently so that you don't bruise his or her ego and make an adversary out of the person in the process.

There's a lot of evidence that shows that social skills can greatly improve your career prospects. There are very few jobs where people are isolated in their own offices; most jobs require teamwork and interpersonal relationships. Today, more than ever, networking is a crucial component of career advancement, and it's a predictor of success in entrepreneurship. To network effectively, you need to have advanced social skills.

Finally, studies show that social skills increase people's overall level of happiness. When you have poor social skills, you find it hard to coexist with people, and that can make you miserable. However, if you develop your social skills, it becomes exponentially easier for you to meet with new people, to have a mature relationship with your partner, to resolve conflicts at home and at work, and to stand up for yourself when you feel that someone is unfair towards you. The end result is that you don't bottle up negative emotions, so you lead a happy and fulfilled life.

CHAPTER 17:

How Social Skills Can Help You Become More Persuasive

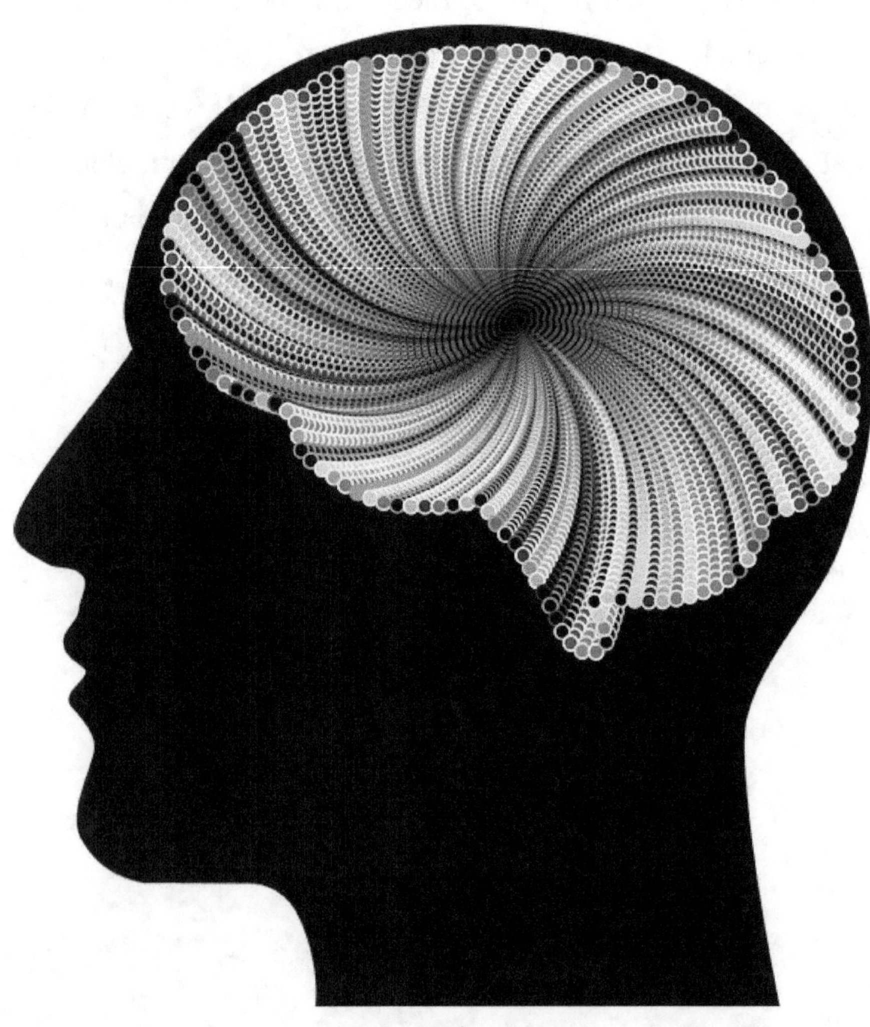

There are several social skills that come in handy when you want to be persuasive. We have mentioned that "social skills" is a broad term that encompasses dozens of other specific skills. Where persuasion is concerned, the applicable social skills include communication skills, conflict management skills, leadership skills, rapport building skills (the ability to bond with people), teamwork, change management skills and many other skills that relate to emotional intelligence.

Social skills can help you be more persuasive by making you good at articulating and relaying your messages. Social skills help you understand the person you are targeting for the purposes of persuasion, and they help you craft an effective communication strategy that will work with that particular person.

When you have good social skills, you understand that social interactions are about the give and take, so if you are seeking to get something from someone, you will take the time to develop a mutually beneficial relationship with him, instead of a one-sided relationship where the person will easily sense that you are trying to take advantage of him.

Most of the time, persuasion involves negotiation. It's rare that you will find someone agreeing to do something you want, without them insisting that you accommodate some of their conditions. So, negotiation is a very crucial social skill when you want to persuade someone. Negotiating is about clarifying your position, acknowledging someone else's position, and then trying to find a middle ground that satisfies both parties. For example, if you are a salesman, the ability to negotiate can help you persuade reluctant customers to buy your products and services, by making them feel as though you are compromising with them, and that they are getting real value out of the deal.

Conflict management and resolution is another social skill that can be extremely useful when you are trying to persuade someone. When you have good conflict resolution skills, you tend to be more tactful and diplomatic in your approach, so you are in a better position to persuade someone to change their minds, even if they have very strong convictions, to begin with.

Conflict management and persuasion have a lot in common (in some cases, they are one and the same things. They both involve bringing disagreements out in the open and then working together to resolve those disagreements. In interpersonal relationships, conflict resolution involves sharing your emotions with the other person and having a healthy debate on how to solve your common problems. If you have mastered this skill, you can apply it whenever you have to persuade someone who is close to you.

Just like the other social skills, we have discussed; leadership skills can also be extremely useful when it comes to persuasion. A person who has good leadership skills is able to articulate a vision that he or she has and to make other people feel enthusiastic about that vision. Having that quality will make you significantly better at persuasion. People with leadership skills also tend to have charisma, which, as we've seen, is crucial when you want to be persuasive.

Having good leadership skills doesn't necessarily mean that you need to be in a formal leadership role; it means that you are able to influence people, to get them to see things your way, and to inspire them to follow your lead.

Building rapport and connecting with people is a social skill that can help set the stage for you to persuade people. We've already mentioned in this book that people are more likely to be persuaded if they feel that they have a connection with you; that just goes to show how vital bonding and rapport-building is as a social skill.

A good rapport is the foundation of a good relationship, so whether you are trying to persuade a total stranger or someone with whom you are well squinted, rapport is very important.

It may not seem so at face value, but teamwork is also a crucial social skill that can help you seem more persuasive. When you are a good team player, the people you interact with feel like you have their backs, and that they can depend on you, so they'll be more inclined to comply when you persuade them to take certain actions. If you are a good teammate to your girlfriend, boyfriend, or spouse, you are better placed to persuade them, because there is a sense of trust and co-dependency between the two of you.

CHAPTER 18:

Use Social Skills to Build an Effective Communication Strategy

So far, we have looked at social skills, and we have explained how they are linked to both communication skills and persuasion strategies. In this chapter, we will focus on how you can use all of these skills to come up with an effective communication strategy.

Since our central focus is persuasion, we will look at effective communication strategies in the context of interpersonal conversations (as opposed to public speaking or mass media communication). So, we will mostly discuss conversation strategies.

Conversations are hard to start, to sustain, and even to conclude, but they get much more complicated when you are trying to persuade someone. Even if you don't have social anxiety, it's still hard to connect with someone and to have a smooth conversation. So, let's look at ways to boost all the stages of a conversation as you create your communication strategy.

The first thing you need to do is identify your conversational trouble spots. If you evaluate your conversations, you may be able to note that there are certain areas where you have hang-ups. Here are a few trouble spots that are common among people with social anxiety: having trouble starting a conversation; running out of things to say in the middle of the conversation; being reluctant to talk about yourself; finding yourself agreeing with the other person or nodding, even if you have a different opinion on the topic.

You can try recalling your recent conversations or monitoring the conversations that you have in the next few days to identify your hang-ups and weak points.

If you have a difficult time starting conversation, there are some things that you can do about it as part of your communication strategy. You can teach yourself to start by bringing up a general topic and steering away from getting too personal with your choice of topic. For instance, you can start by talking about the weather, or what a nice day it is. There are lots of small-talk topics that you can opt to, and these topics are very effective when it comes to breaking the ice.

You can also start a conversation by paying the other person a compliment. If you don't have a close personal relationship with the person, it's better to keep the compliment as general as possible because you don't want the person to get sensitive and to close himself off. You can say things like "that jumper looks nice." You want to avoid using compliments that could be inappropriate, given the context.

A great way to start a conversation is by making a general observation about a person and then getting him to talk more about that topic. If you notice that the person has a unique item of clothing that could be your way in; just tell him or her how nice you think it is, and where you might get it if you wanted to purchase a similar item. If the person is holding a phone, ask about the brand, how well they like using it, and whether they would recommend it to you.

One of the reasons many of us find it hard to start a conversation is that we keep racking our brains for something witty to say. The problem with witty statements is that most people aren't good with impromptu wit, so they end up getting stuck, or they find themselves saying something out loud only to realize that it doesn't sound as good as it did in the head. If you like to use witty statements as conversation starters, you need to put in a lot of practice. However, the better option is just to focus on using sincere and genuine statements as conversation starters.

After breaking the ice, you should quickly transition into your intended topic of conversation. That's because people tend to have a very short attention span, and if you waste too much time with small-talk, the moment will pass, and you might not get to say what you want.

You can tell how receptive a person is to your topic of conversation by observing their non-verbal cues. We have talked about how to read people in an earlier chapter in this book, but even without any training, you might be able to tell if someone is interested in what you have to say, or if he finds it uncomfortable to keep talking about that given topic.

In order to keep a conversation going, you have to remember that it's a two-way street. Even if you initiate a conversation because you are trying to persuade the person to do something, you shouldn't make the conversation all about you.

Try to create continuity in the conversation. That means that you should avoid responses that are likely to shut down the conversation. When conversing, use open-ended questions instead of close-ended ones. Avoid phrasing questions in such a way that you get yes or no answers. Instead, set the tone for the other person to speak more widely about himself. Remember that the more the person opens up, the more you get to know about them, so the more information you have at your disposal to use to persuade them.

You should also try to be aware of certain mannerisms that you have, and you should try to control them during a conversation. For example, you might notice that you tend to talk too much when you are nervous, or that you get excited and your tone changes when you get to a topic about which you are passionate. When you want to persuade someone, you want to come across as composed and in control of your emotions.

In as much as you might be able to create and execute a conversation strategy, the best way to improve your conversation skills is through practice. Start conversations with strangers whenever you can, and practice giving people compliments.

CHAPTER 19:

What Is Emotional Competence (EC)?

The term emotional competence refers to the ability of a person to freely express his or her emotions. Emotional competence is closely related to emotional intelligence; in fact, some books tend to use the two terms interchangeably. The word competence implies having a certain level of skill in the way you express your emotion, and in your awareness of how your emotions affect people around you.

Emotional competence also has a lot to do with one's ability to control their emotions, and to adapt when they are subjected to emotionally challenging situations. Emotional competence focuses more on understanding oneself than on figuring out other people's emotions.

There are lots of documented reasons why emotional competent is important. People who lack emotional competence tend to suppress their emotions instead of expressing them and sharing them with the people in their lives. In doing so, they often end up getting depressed, or in other cases, their relationships become toxic because of their bottled-up emotions. If you are emotionally incompetent, your relationships with other people will suffer.

So, how can you tell if you have emotional competence? Well, one can be considered to be emotionally competent if he or she is able to handle emotionally-demanding situations and activities, including sharing feelings, relating well with others, showing flexibility in a relationship, being able to express intimacy, being able to handle disagreements, being able to manage expectations, and being able to forgive others.

 So far, we have discussed the first two indicators of emotional competence (expressing feelings, and relating well with others), so let's talk briefly about the other indicators.

Flexibility refers to the quality of being able to switch from playing the role of the stronger person to playing the role of the weaker person in a relationship. When you are in a functional relationship with someone, you go back and forth; there are times when you have to lean on the other person, and there are times when the other person has to lean on you. If you lack flexibility, it either means that you want to be the strong one all the time, or you want to be the weak one all the time. in such cases, the relationship can quickly turn toxic because you will either be perceived as controlling (if you always want to be stronger) or you will be perceived as clingy (if you always want to be weaker).

Intimacy is the quality of being comfortable with close sexual and non-sexual contact (e.g., cuddling, sharing inner thoughts, etc.).

The ability to deal with disagreement is about being able to let the other person in the partnership have a different opinion from yours without having to try to control each other or to engage in a power struggle.

Managing expectations is about being able to adjust your attitude without despairing if you find yourself (or your partner) falling short in one way or another.

Forgiveness is about being able to acknowledge that you and others have weaknesses and that it's better to let things go than to live with resentment.

CHAPTER 20:

Emotional Competence in Relationships

Without emotional competence, relationships become harder to manage, and we are more likely to find ourselves losing the special bond that we have with our partners, as the relationship turns increasingly toxic. Romantic relationships are primarily characterized by emotions. In other relationship dynamics (e.g., working relationships or friendships), there is an emotional involvement between the two parties, but to a lesser extent – so emotional competence may not be as crucial in such case, but it's still extremely important.

No relationship can succeed if the people involved don't make an effort to handle their emotions and channel them in a constructive way. Let's look at how you can increase your emotional competence in order to improve your relationship.

First, you have to know yourself. The foundation of emotional competence is understanding yourself and your emotional tendencies. You have to understand how you come across to the people around you, especially those with whom you are closely related. You need to figure you're your strengths, areas where you could stand to improve, things, or situations that have the ability to trigger you and elicit negative emotional reactions, and your own values. If you know yourself, you can have a frank discussion with your partner about your emotional strengths and weaknesses, so that they can help you regulate yourself.

Secondly, you have to often yourself up so that you are more receptive to criticism and other forms of feedback. Emotional competence in the context of a relationship is often about taking in the feedback that your partner gives you so that you can grow together. You have to remember that there are two people in that relationship, both of whom have emotional needs that are equally important, so accepting constructive criticism will help you have smoother and more fulfilling relationships.

However, you also have to be cautious so that you can tell the difference between constructive criticism and negative criticism. When your partner offers constructive criticism, they make suggestions that could improve your life. When he or she offers negative criticism, they are trying to change you on a level that is so fundamental that you may lose your identity in the process. Being able to distinguish between these two kinds of criticism can save you from ending up in a relationship where the other person controls you.

You can also use emotional competence to improve your relationship by taking steps to build intimacy. Intimacy is what makes any relationship strong, which is why it's a vital component of emotional competence.

There are lots of ways to increase intimacy. First, you can disclose more information about yourself to your partner, and you can actively encourage your partner to talk to you about how he or she is feeling. Try to make time to have deep emotional conversations at the end of the day. This may involve ensuring that you go to bed together at the same time every day (incidentally, if the two of you go to bed at different times, it could be a sign of diminishing intimacy). You can also try to take on new projects or hobbies together with your partner.

Emotional competence, as we mentioned in the previous chapter, is also about flexibility. To improve your relationship, you need to introduce some flexibility in it. Many psychologists have pointed out that flexibility is one of the most underrated relationship skills out there.

Flexibility means being ready to let go of convictions, ideas, and things. The opposite of flexibility is rigidity, and where there's rigidity in a relationship, there is no compromise. In a relationship, you need to show flexibility by letting go of the idea that you have the mandate to control every aspect of the relationship. Chances are you will have a partner who doesn't share some of your values and beliefs; in such a case, you have to find the middle ground.

Flexibility is also letting go of the need to always be right. Insisting on "being right" might serve you well in your career or your business, but it's not a good thing in a relationship. If you always want to be right when you have debates with your partner, that's the same thing as saying that your partner is always wrong, and that definitely won't sit well with him or her. If you are set on winning every argument with your partner, the two of you will start being competitors instead of teammates, and it's just a matter of time before one of you turns resentful, bitter, or vindictive. So, the next time you want to show your partner how right you are, ask yourself "at what cost?"

In as much as flexibility is important in a relationship, it's unwise to compromise on the principles and values that are most dear to you, so you are better off finding a partner who shares those values in the first place instead of getting into a relationship with someone who doesn't and trying to change them.

CHAPTER 21:

Win Friends with Social Leverage

When we hear the word leverage, it's often in the context of financial investing, international trade, and transactional relationships. Social leverage is somewhat similar to financial leverage (they have the same working principle). The difference is in whatever acts as capital: in financial leverage, money is the capital. In social leverage, relationships are the capital. Social leverage refers to any positive human interaction that you can channel to get a useful outcome, including gaining information, creating future opportunities, or even fulfilling emotional needs.

Social leverage is sometimes referred to as social capital. It comprises of a broad range of things, including interpersonal relationships, the sense of kinship, shared values, shared identities, shared norms, established trust, previous cooperation, a sense of obligation, and reciprocity.

Social leverage or capital could be anything that could give you an upper hand in your interaction with someone. Let's say for example that you go for an interview, and one or more of the panelists went to the same college as you; it might not seem significant at face value, but that shared identity can turn out to be the crucial social leverage that you need to edge out your competitors and win the position for which you are interviewing.

If you understand the concept of social leverage, you will be amazed at how useful it can be. Any minor social connection can be leveraged to create a greater, more meaningful, or even profitable connection. Businesses use social leverage to increase their customer bases all the time. for example, if you open a restaurant in town and you want to attract more customers, you can use social leverage by sponsoring the little-league soccer team at a nearby school, and soon enough, people are going to start seeing your business as a pillar of the community, and they'll quickly turn into patrons.

You can easily win friends using social leverage. If you have just one mutual friend with someone, then you have the ability to use social leverage to win over that person and turn him or her into a friend. Even if you don't have many friends, to begin with, you can quickly expand your circle of friends by pursuing friendships with your friends' friends.

The best way to meet potential friends is to attend every social event to which you are invited. Make the time to go to birthday parties, office parties, hangouts, etc. These days, with social media platforms and the internet in general, it's very easy to receive invitations to one form of gathering or the other, so we tend to ignore them most of the time, but if you want to build friendships, going to those events is the best way to find viable candidates.

In the context of a career or a business, you can gain social leverage and win acquaintances by attending networking events. Networking is the process of interacting with people with the deliberate intention of creating professional or social contacts, which you may be able to leverage at a future date. You may also network with the intention of gaining more information about players in your industry and trends in your business.

You can also win friends by leveraging whatever social pull you have at the moment. Whatever your position in society is right now, it has certain tangible or intangible values to different people around you; with a bit of tact, you can use that position to gain friends and to expand your social circle.

No matter how lowly or inconsequential you think your position might be, there are ways to use that position to build relationships with people, businesses, organizations, etc. that could offer you something of value in return.

Take the position of a student, for example. If you tell someone that you are a student, they may not think much of it, but the truth is that you can gain an audience with CEOs of big companies or even high-level government officials just by claiming that you are a student who needs to interview them for a school newspaper, or even for a college credit assignment. So, it's not a question of how big your current standing in society is, it's just a question of how aggressive you are in your use of social leverage.

You can use social leverage, not just to make friends, but to meet the kind of people that can help you with career progression or even social mobility. If you don't have much social leverage, to begin with, it's possible to pull it out of thin air; remember that most of the time, social leverage seems intangible until you use it. Let's say, for example, that you want to add influential people to your network, but you don't have a high enough status to move in their circles. You might be able to use social leverage to get access to them. If you want to meet CEOs of companies, you can register your own company, name yourself CEO, and that will be your ticket into the CEO club; even if your company isn't worth much, you can honestly claim to be a member of that group of elites.

CHAPTER 22:

10 Social Skills That Are Essential for Success in Business and Relationships

In this book, we have defined social skills as a set of techniques that people can use to start, develop, and leverage relationships with other people. These days, people are increasingly taking social skills for granted. Thanks to technology, we are more focused on interacting with people over the internet, so we put less stock on practicing your social skills, but that doesn't mean that they are any less important than they were a few years back. In this chapter, we will discuss 10 of the essential social skills that you need to develop if you want to succeed, whether it's in your personal life, or in your business or career.

Maintaining Eye Contact During Conversations

Maintaining eye contact can go a long way in improving your personal and business relationships alike. When you maintain eye contact with someone with who you are in business, you come across as more confident and therefore more authoritative, so they are more likely to take you seriously.

When you hold eye contact with people in your personal life, they are more likely to pay attention to what you say, and they are more likely to think of you as credible. So, if you are going on a first date, maintaining eye contact actually increases the likelihood that the person will take you seriously as a potential suitor.

When you start making eye contact with people, it's going to feel a bit uncomfortable at first, but the more you practice, they more comfortable you will get at doing it.

It's important to make a distinction between eye contact and glaring; a glare involves eye contact, but it's accompanied by facial expressions that indicate contempt or anger. You should also be tactful about the way you use eye contact. Holding eye contact for a long time with a romantic partner is okay; in fact, studies show that it increases intimacy. However, if you hold eye contact for long with a stranger, or with someone in a professional situation, he or she will feel intimidated. For long interactions, try to hold eye contact, but break it at least once every minute to keep the person from interpreting it as a sign of aggression.

Use the Right Body Language

You can use body language to make people feel comfortable around you, to create connections with people, to stress certain points in business meetings, etc. No matter who you meet, whether it's a business or a personal relationship, you want to use body language to create a good impression and to open up the communication channels between you and the person in question.

You can use various body language signals to indicate confidence. For example, if you start a conversation with a firm handshake, the person will subconsciously take it an indication of the strength of character. A weak handshake, on the other hand, can prime the other person to assume that you are a weak individual.

Posture is a major component of body language, and you need to practice good posture if you want to make a great first impression on whomever you meet. You want to have a posture that's related, but not slouched. As you learn a new posture, you will have to consciously adjust your posture for a while before it becomes habitual. Always stand up straight and carry yourself around with your head held high.

Body language also includes the use of hand gestures and arm placement. You need to pay attention to the way you position our hands when you talk to people. In public speaking, you can use your hands to stress certain points and to improve the overall quality of your communication technique.

Understanding the Difference Between Assertiveness and Being Aggressive

Many people have a problem being assertive because they don't want to be perceived as aggressive. Some other people act aggressively while assuming that they are assertive, often to their detriment. Understanding the difference between these two terms will make it possible for you to properly utilize one of the most important social skills.

Being assertive is about standing up for yourself and asking to be treated fairly. Being aggressive is about lashing out with negative emotions in response to treatment that you think is unfair.

When you are assertive, it means that you value yourself, and you fundamentally believe that you are equal to others. Your goal isn't to gain the upper hand over someone else; it is to make sure that everyone gets their fair share of respect, including yourself. Assertiveness is not about being self-centered, or being a bully; it's about expressing your needs to the other party so that they are fairly taken into account. On the other hand, aggressiveness is about valuing yourself more than other people.

When you are assertive, your goal isn't to cause harm to anyone. The reason assertiveness is often confused with aggressiveness is that sometimes people react to both in the same manner. When someone wants to take advantage of you, and you assert for yourself, he may react in an aggressive or defensive way. It's not possible for you to control how others react, but at the very list, you may be able to work on your delivery when you are assertive.

When you assert for yourself, you should express your opinion as clearly, concisely, and diplomatically as possible. You want to be very clear so that there is little room for a willful misunderstanding from the other party. At the same time, you want to foster mutual respect and to create a working relationship with the other person, so you should avoid using language that will deliberately offend the person.

Selecting the Most Effective Communication Channels at Your Disposal

There are many different ways to communicate, but if you want to have a great business and personal relationships, you need to be very particular about the communication channels that you use. These days, it's very easy to communicate through messaging, emails, and social media posts, but you have to ask yourself, "is that the most effective way for me to relay my message?"

For example, if you criticize someone (e.g., a coworker, a friend, or a family member), writing them an email is extremely unwise. If you deal with any kind of conflict over a messaging service, it always leaves a bad taste in the mouth of the recipient of your message. Additionally, there is always the chance that your message could get in the wrong hands or it could be taken out of context, and that won't make you look good.

Criticizing people or arguing with them through messages can be seen as a sign of cowardice. It's better to meet people face to face if you have any grievances that you need to relay. That way, they have the opportunity to defend themselves, and you are more likely to come to an amicable solution while maintaining mutual respect.

Being Flexible and Cooperative

It's impossible to foster good personal and professional relationships if you have the attitude that you are always right, and anyone with a contrary opinion is always wrong. There is no relationship that can succeed if one person has a "my way or the highway" attitude; even if you are the boss and the other person is your employee, it's better to have a meeting of the minds instead of just dictating terms to the other person.

Even if you are confident that you are right, always be ready to cooperate with people and to find ways to accommodate their needs. Sometimes, it's not just about being right; it's about making everyone feel like they have a say or a stake in the relationship. If you have a flexible mindset, you will create a dynamic where everyone feels free to share their ideas, and the relationship will be stronger for that reason.

Being Able to Accept Constructive Criticisms

When we are criticized, our natural response is to be defensive and to push back. That kind of conditioning is hard to overcome, and it takes a lot of willpower to learn to accept constructive criticism. Whether it's in your personal life or at work, you need to learn to listen to what other people are saying, to consider their idea in its entirety, to make an objective judgment as to whether the idea is constructive or not, and to respond graciously without lashing out defensively.

You should take criticism seriously, whether or not it was solicited. When you accept criticism, you acknowledge the fact that you are a human being who is prone to error, and that the people around you aren't necessarily malicious; some of them mean you well.

However, as a point of caution, you need to train yourself to tell the difference between the kind of criticism that builds you up, and the kind that is carefully crafted by a malicious person to tear you down. Constructive criticism often comes with suggestions on how you can improve. However, the kind of criticism that is done out of malice often fail to identify probable solutions, and it instead focuses on blowing your shortcomings out of proportion.

Irrespective of what kind of criticism you receive, don't take it personally. Incorporate the good advice, and let go of the bad advice.

Staying Positive Through Challenging Situations

Life can throw lots of challenges at you, and when things get overwhelming, it becomes extremely easy for you to throw in the towel. Remaining positive in the face of challenges is a very crucial social skill to have because everything in life is a challenge.

You will find it challenging to start and maintain close personal relationships. Your business relationships may be antagonistic by nature, and your job may involve a lot of pushback between you and your coworkers or your boss. If you have a challenging career, you may have to deal with projects that overwhelm you. If you can't stay positive, you will not be able to succeed at anything.

This is the social skill that makes it possible for you to stay motivated and to see things through. It's a skill that helps you to win the heart of a romantic interest who is reluctant to date you at first. It's a skill that helps you stay on course as an entrepreneur even though you make losses in the first few quarters.

Being a Good Learner

Our world most at a very fast pace today, and trends change quickly both in business and in society. That means that you have to keep learning if you want to survive in the current business arena. To be a successful entrepreneur, you have to constantly learn new concepts and adopt new business practices.

Being a good learner is also important if you want to quickly pick you knew social skills. You need to have a hunger for knowledge, and you need to be eternally curious about how people think, feel, and behave, and what motivates them.

The desire to learn is important if you want to be an expert on anything, and that applies both in your career and in your life. If you want to be an expert at parenting, you have to learn to be one. If you want to be an expert at dating or marriage, you need to take in as much information as you can.

Respecting Others

Respect it the one social skill that makes you noble. When you respect others, they'll respect you in return.

One thing you need to understand about life, is that it's filled with ups and downs, so if you find yourself on top of the pyramid (e.g., if you are the boss, or if you are wealthy), respecting others is the only way to ensure that you have allies on your side if the tide turns.

There is also a self-serving component to the notion of respecting others; it can boost your self-esteem. When you respect others, you are working off the premise that you are not better than other people, and that everyone, despite their current station, is deserving of respect. If that's a core belief that you have, then you will automatically extend that respect onto yourself, and you won't ever experience low self-esteem.

Being Yourself

Surprisingly, many people lack this social skill, even though it sounds like something that people should naturally understand. Being yourself means having your own unique identity and keeping others from usurping that identity.

Being yourself means that you are secure, confident, and willing to let other people see the real you. It means that when you get into a relationship, the other person sees the true you and either accepts or rejects you based on that, instead of a fake curated image of yourself.

These days, authenticity is a rare but valuable commodity, so it can go a long way in helping you succeed, both in business and in life.

CHAPTER 23:

Empathy and Emotional Intelligence at Work

Earlier in the book, we defined emotional intelligence as a person's ability to perceive, understand and manage their own emotions and the emotions of others, and we pointed out that empathy was one of the 5 main components of emotional intelligence. Here, we want to look at emotional intelligence (EI) in the context of a workplace environment.

Emotional intelligence is important in the workplace for any number of reasons, but the bottom line is that the workplace is a social environment with lots of interpersonal dynamics, so everything works better when people understand their emotions, and they can empathize with others.

There are lots of studies that link emotional intelligence with job satisfaction. Emotionally intelligent people enjoy their jobs more than those with lower levels of emotional intelligence. Additionally, people seem to like their jobs better when they work under the supervision of someone who is emotionally intelligent. In general, EI is strongly associated with job performance.

Emotionally intelligent people tend to be more productive because they are in a better position to stay motivated and to work harder on all tasks.

Emotionally intelligent people perform well at work because they are emotionally stable. This means that they are able to tolerate high levels of stress. Where others can let stress turn into anxiety or depression, emotionally intelligent people can control the stress and channel it into productive energy.

Emotionally intelligent people also do well at work because they tend to be more conscientious. Conscientiousness refers to a person's tendency to respect social norms, to work diligently, to control their impulses, etc. In the workplace, conscientious people are more likely to follow their employers' instructions, and they are more inclined to feel guilty if their performance declines, so they tend to put in more effort.

Emotionally intelligent people also do well at work because they generally tend to be extraverted. Extroverts are best suited for jobs that require a lot of teamwork and interactions because they tend to thrive in a social environment. Introverts, on the other hand, do better when they have jobs that require them to work alone. So, extraversion is only an indicator of job performance as long as long as you are dealing with a job that requires interactions (that describes the vast majority of jobs in the world today).

If the majority of people in a workplace or most of the employees in a business have high emotional intelligence, researchers have found that such places are characterized by high levels of motivation; a powerful sense of common vision; a high level of adaptability (where the company is quick to change with the market); clear interpersonal communication (which ensures that everyone is always on the same page, ideas are openly shared, and they are adapted based on merit, and employees feel heard and respected); and high levels of self-leadership (where all team members are driven to take the initiative, and they perform with minimum supervision).

If you have a workplace where many people lack emotional intelligence, you might easily end up with a dysfunctional system. Studies show that low levels of EI in the workplace often leads to poor communication, which can affect the performance of the entire team. There is also a lot of evidence which shows that decision making is negatively impacted by low EI in the workplace.

Remember that when people have low EI, they have a low understanding of their own emotions, and an even lower understanding of other people's emotions. When such people are put together in teams, the problem can compound, and it won't be long until you have a dysfunctional team where people don't get along. You will experience many incidences of emotional outbursts, and you might find yourself with a team where everyone hates each other's guts, and ultimately, productivity will suffer.

Low EI affects decision making in the workplace because if you have people that don't understand each other's emotions, then the organization can't deal with interpersonal issues, and it can't adequately factor the cause and effect relationship between events that occur and people's emotions. They'll always make decisions that fail to accommodate some people's emotional needs, and those decisions will be detrimental to the collective group.

When you are a decision-maker at work, you can't just focus on the numbers; you have to understand people's emotions. For example, if you want to increase your output, you might push your team members to meet higher quarters, but fail to consider the fact that the added pressure may cause stress and anxiety in your teammates, and that the net effect might be that their performance actually declines. Your teammates (the ones with low EI), will not be able to cope with anxiety, and they may start making irrational decisions, and that could end up affecting the bottom line of the organization.

CHAPTER 24:

How to Improve Business Relationships

The business world today is much more complex than it was a decade ago because of advancements in technology. The faced-paced nature of these advancements makes it somewhat difficult to remember what drives businesses towards success. You might have a business that heavily relies on the use of software, the use of machines, the use of social media, etc., but ultimately, your success as a business person or as an entrepreneur depends on the strength of your business relationships.

Many psychologists have noted that business relationships aren't that much different from personal relationships; although such relationships are generally more professional, and there is less emotional involvement between the two parties, most of the time, the core dynamics remain the same. Whereas personal relationships fulfill emotional needs, business relationships fulfill financial needs; other than that, they are basically similar.

The first thing you need to do to improve your business relationships is to create a system to manage and nurture those relationships. Just like personal relationships, business relationships take work. The problem with business is that you are always busy, and oftentimes, you don't have time to attend to the relationships. For example, if you are having a hectic month, you might easily forget to call, email, or meet with important clients, suppliers, partners, etc. You may only remember to get in touch with them when there is a problem, but by then, the quality of your relationship might have deteriorated.

To avoid such scenarios, you have to come up with a system that allows you to make time for your business relationships, even if things get busy. You can schedule regular meetings in your colander so that you don't overlook the relationships. You can also try to figure out how your customers, business partners, and employees want to be treated, and you should set standards on how to handle the relationships.

You can also improve your business relationships by making the other person feel special. If you are trying to win a client, you can woo him using techniques that are similar to the kinds you use in romantic relationships. People like relationships that make them feel special and that doesn't change even if it's a business relationship.

The people with who you do business are aware of the fact that you are always busy, and you have lots of responsibility, so if you make time for them, and if you go the extra mile to attend to them, they'll get the sense that they are important to you.

Reciprocity is very important in business, so one of the best ways to improve your business relationships is by giving as much as you expect. Think of what you put into a business relationship as an investment. You expect your investment to pay off through reciprocity. If you invest in building a strong relationship with a customer, you expect customer loyalty in return. If you build a strong relationship with your suppliers, you expect reliability in return. The more attention you put into the relationship, the bigger your return. So, don't make a half-hearted effort to nurture business relationships; make sure that your clients really believe that they are a priority.

You also want to build business relationships that have the effect of diversifying your networks. In as much as you want to maintain your current relationships, you always need to be able to expand your circle to pave the way for the growth of your business. For example, if you have a relationship with one supplier, you might want to get to know other suppliers so that you have backups in case your current one is unable to fulfill your orders. You should also expand your network beyond your current industry, and try to build relationships with relevant people in other organizations. You might want to be friendly with government officials, local law enforcement, the local media, community organizations, etc.

One highly effective way to improve your business relationships is to channel some of your resources towards helping with community projects or dealing with social issues. You want everyone you associate with to think of you as a pillar of the community, and as a generous person who cares about everyone's welfare.

Conclusion

Thanks for making it through to the end of *Psychology of Persuasion: Secrets to Influence People & Human Behavior with Dark Cognitive Therapy, CBT, & Emotional Intelligence; Win Friends Using Social Leverage, Empathy, and Business Relationship Skills.* I hope that you have learned effective techniques and skills that can help you be more persuasive as you navigate through life.

The next step is to start practicing the persuasion techniques, communication skills, social skills, and CBT strategies that you have learned in this book. Practicing is the key to mastering any skill, so it's not just enough to read this book; for each technique we have described here, try to picture yourself using it in the real world. Whenever the opportunity presents itself, just put one of the tricks you've acquired here into play, and see how it turns out.

After practicing for a while, these persuasion techniques will come naturally to you, and they'll feel like second nature. When this happens, life will be much more enjoyable. You will be able to influence people on a whim, and lots of doors will be opened to you as a result.

As you master these skills, remember that they are powerful tools, so try to avoid using them to exploit people. When you have the power to effectively persuade anyone, then you essentially have the ability to control people's lives; try to use these techniques for the common good.

www.ingramcontent.com/pod-product-compliance
Lightning Source LLC
Chambersburg PA
CBHW061807250726

48657CB00001B/327